UTOPIA OF USURERS

AND OTHER ESSAYS

G. K. Chesterton

Wiseblood Classics of Philosophy

Milwaukee, Wisconsin

www.wisebloodbooks.com

First Published in 1917
Printed in the United States of America Set in Arabic Typesetting

Library of Congress Cataloging-in-Publication Data Chesterton,
Gilbert Keith, 1874-1936
Utopia of Usurers and Other Essays
1. Chesterton, G.K., 1874-1936—essays 2. Economics—Usury
3. Religion 4. Imperialism 5. Journalistic Criticism

ISBN: 978-1-951319-67-0

Table of Contents

Extra, Extra!

A SONG OF SWORDS

"A drove of cattle came into a village called Swords;
and was stopped by the rioters." —Daily Paper.

In the place called Swords on the Irish road
It is told for a new renown
How we held the horns of the cattle, and how
We will hold the horns of the devils now
Ere the lord of hell with the horn on his brow
Is crowned in Dublin town.

Light in the East and light in the West,
And light on the cruel lords,
On the souls that suddenly all men knew,
And the green flag flew and the red flag flew,
And many a wheel of the world stopped, too,
When the cattle were stopped at Swords.

Be they sinners or less than saints
That smite in the street for rage,
We know where the shame shines bright; we know
You that they smite at, you their foe,
Lords of the lawless wage and low,
This is your lawful wage.

You pinched a child to a torture price
That you dared not name in words;
So black a jest was the silver bit
That your own speech shook for the shame of it,
And the coward was plain as a cow they hit
When the cattle have strayed at Swords.

The wheel of the torrent of wives went round
To break men's brotherhood;
You gave the good Irish blood to grease
The clubs of your country's enemies;
you saw the brave man beat to the knees:
And you saw that it was good.

The rope of the rich is long and long—
The longest of hangmen's cords;
But the kings and crowds are holding their breath,
In a giant shadow o'er all beneath
Where God stands holding the scales of Death
Between the cattle and Swords.

Haply the lords that hire and lend
The lowest of all men's lords,
Who sell their kind like kine at a fair,
Will find no head of their cattle there;
But faces of men where cattle were:
Faces of men—and Swords.

UTOPIA OF USURERS

I. Art and Advertisement

I propose, subject to the patience of the reader, to devote two or three articles to prophecy. Like all healthy-minded prophets, sacred and profane, I can only prophesy when I am in a rage and think things look ugly for everybody. And like all healthy-minded prophets, I prophesy in the hope that my prophecy may not come true. For the prediction made by the true soothsayer is like the warning given by a good doctor. And the doctor has really triumphed when the patient he condemned to death has revived to life. The threat is justified at the very moment when it is falsified. Now I have said again and again (and I shall continue to say again and again on all the most inappropriate occasions) that we must hit Capitalism, and hit it hard, for the plain and definite reason that it is growing stronger. Most of the excuses which serve the capitalists as masks are, of course, the excuses of hypocrites. They lie when they claim philanthropy; they no more feel any particular love of men than Albu felt an affection for Chinamen. They lie when they say they have reached their position through their own organising ability. They generally have to pay men to organise the mine, exactly as they pay men to go down it. They often lie about the present wealth, as they generally lie about their past poverty. But when they say that they are going in for a "constructive social policy," they do not lie. They really are going in for a constructive social policy. And we must go in for an equally destructive social policy; and destroy, while it is still half-constructed, the accursed thing which they construct.

The Example of the Arts

Now I propose to take, one after another, certain aspects and departments of modern life, and describe what I think they will be like in this paradise of plutocrats, this Utopia of gold and brass in which the great story of England seems so likely to end. I propose to say what I think our new masters, the mere millionaires, will do with certain human interests and institutions, such as art, science, jurisprudence, or religion—unless we strike soon enough to prevent them. And for the sake of argument I will take in this article the example of the arts.

Most people have seen a picture called "Bubbles," which is used for the advertisement of a celebrated soap, a small cake of which is introduced into the pictorial design. And anybody with an instinct for design (the caricaturist of the Daily Herald, for instance), will guess that it was not originally a part of the design. He will see that the cake of soap destroys the picture as a picture; as much as if the cake of soap had been used to Scrub off the paint. Small as it is, it breaks and confuses the whole balance of objects in the composition. I offer no judgment here upon Millais's action in the matter; in fact, I do not know what it was. The important point for me at the moment is that the picture was not painted for the soap, but the soap added to the picture. And the spirit of the corrupting change which has separated us from that Victorian epoch can be best seen in this: that the Victorian atmosphere, with all its faults, did not permit such a style of patronage to pass as a matter of course. Michael Angelo may have been proud to have helped an emperor or a pope; though, indeed, I think he was prouder than they were on his own account. I do not believe Sir John Millais was proud of having helped a soap-boiler. I do not say he thought it wrong; but he was not proud of it. And that marks precisely the change from his time to our own. Our merchants have really adopted the style of merchant princes. They have begun openly to dominate the civilisation of the State, as the emperors and popes openly dominated in Italy. In Millais's time, broadly speaking, art was supposed to mean good art;

advertisement was supposed to mean inferior art. The head of a black man, painted to advertise somebody's blacking, could be a rough symbol, like an inn sign. The black man had only to be black enough. An artist exhibiting the picture of a negro was expected to know that a black man is not so black as he is painted. He was expected to render a thousand tints of grey and brown and violet: for there is no such thing as a black man just as there is no such thing as a white man. A fairly clear line separated advertisement from art.

The First Effect

I should say the first effect of the triumph of the capitalist (if we allow him to triumph) will be that that line of demarcation will entirely disappear. There will be no art that might not just as well be advertisement. I do not necessarily mean that there will be no good art; much of it might be, much of it already is, very good art. You may put it, if you please, in the form that there has been a vast improvement in advertisements. Certainly there would be nothing surprising if the head of a negro advertising Somebody's Blacking now adays were finished with as careful and subtle colours as one of the old and superstitious painters would have wasted on the negro king who brought gifts to Christ. But the improvement of advertisements is the degradation of artists. It is their degradation for this clear and vital reason: that the artist will work, not only to please the rich, but only to increase their riches; which is a considerable step lower. After all, it was as a human being that a pope took pleasure in a cartoon of Raphael or a prince took pleasure in a statuette of Cellini. The prince paid for the statuette; but he did not expect the statuette to pay him. It is my impression that no cake of soap can be found anywhere in the cartoons which the Pope ordered of Raphael. And no one who knows the small-minded cynicism of our plutocracy, its secrecy, its gambling spirit, its contempt of conscience, can doubt that the artist-advertiser will often be assisting enterprises over which he will have no moral control, and of which he could feel no moral approval. He will be working to spread quack medicines, queer investments; and will work for Marconi instead of Medici. And to this base ingenuity he will have to bend the proudest and purest of the virtues of the intellect, the power to attract his brethren, and the noble duty of praise. For that picture by Millais is a very allegorical picture. It is almost a prophecy of what uses are awaiting the beauty of the child unborn. The praise will be of a kind that may correctly be called soap; and the enterprises of a kind that may truly be described as Bubbles.

II. Letters and the New Laureates

In these articles I only take two or three examples of the first and fundamental fact of our time. I mean the fact that the capitalists of our community are becoming quite openly the kings of it. In my last (and first) article, I took the case of Art and advertisement. I pointed out that Art must be growing worse—merely because advertisement is growing better. In those days Millais condescended to Pears' soap. In these days I really think it would be Pears who condescended to Millais. But here I turn to an art I know more about, that of journalism. Only in my ease the art verges on artlessness.

The great difficulty with the English lies in the absence of something one may call democratic imagination. We find it easy to realise an individual, but very hard to realise that the great masses consist of individuals. Our system has been aristocratic: in the special sense of there being only a few actors on the stage. And the back scene is kept quite dark, though it is really a throng of faces. Home Rule tended to be not so much the Irish as the Grand Old Man. The Boer War tended not to be so much South Africa as simply "Joe." And it is the amusing but distressing fact that every class of political leadership, as it comes to the front in its turn, catches the rays of this isolating lime-light; and becomes a small aristocracy. Certainly no one has the aristocratic complaint so badly as the Labour Party. At the recent Congress, the real difference between Larkin and the English Labour leaders was not so much in anything right or wrong in what he said, as in something elemental and even mystical in the way he suggested a mob. But it must be plain, even to those who agree with the more official policy, that for Mr. Havelock Wilson the principal question was Mr. Havelock Wilson; and that Mr. Sexton was mainly considering the dignity and fine feelings of Mr. Sexton. You may say they were as sensitive as aristocrats, or as sulky as babies; the point is that the feeling was personal. But Larkin, like Danton, not only talks like ten thousand men talking, but he also has some of the carelessness of the colossus of Arcis; "Que mon nom soit fletri, que la France soit libre."

A Dance of Degradation

It is needless to say that this respecting of persons has led all the other parties a dance of degradation. We ruin South Africa because it would be a slight on Lord Gladstone to save South Africa. We have a bad army, because it would be a snub to Lord Haldane to have a good army. And no Tory is allowed to say "Marconi" for fear Mr. George should say "Kynoch." But this curious personal element, with its appalling lack of patriotism, has appeared in a new and curious form in another department of life; the department of literature, especially periodical literature. And the form it takes is the next example I shall give of the way in which the capitalists are now appearing, more and more openly, as the masters and princes of the community.

I will take a Victorian instance to mark the change; as I did in the case of the advertisement of "Bubbles." It was said in my childhood, by the more apoplectic and elderly sort of Tory, that W. E. Gladstone was only a Free Trader because he had a partnership in Gilbey's foreign wines. This was, no doubt, nonsense; but it had a dim symbolic, or mainly prophetic, truth in it. It was true, to some extent even then, and it has been increasingly true since, that the statesman was often an ally of the salesman; and represented not only a nation of shopkeepers, but one particular shop. But in Gladstone's time, even if this was true, it was never the whole truth; and no one would have endured it being the admitted truth. The politician was not solely an eloquent and persuasive bagman travelling for certain business men; he was bound to mix even his corruption with some intelligible ideals and rules of policy. And the proof of it is this: that at least it was the statesman who bulked large in the public eye; and his financial backer was entirely in the background. Old gentlemen might choke over their port, with the moral certainty that the Prime Minister had shares in a wine merchant's. But the old gentleman would have died on the spot if the wine merchant had really been made as important as the Prime Minister. If it had been Sir Walter Gilbey whom Disraeli denounced, or Punch caricatured; if Sir Walter Gilbey's favourite collars (with the design of which I am unacquainted) had grown as large as the wings of an archangel; if Sir Walter Gilbey had been credited with successfully eliminating the British Oak with his little hatchet; if, near the Temple and the Courts of Justice, our sight was struck by a majestic statue of a wine merchant; or if the earnest Conservative lady who threw a gingerbread-nut at the Premier had directed it towards the wine merchant instead, the shock to Victorian England would have been very great indeed.

Haloes for Employers

Now something very like that is happening; the mere wealthy employer is beginning to have not only the power but some of the glory. I have seen in several magazines lately, and magazines of a high class, the appearance of a new kind of article. Literary men are being employed to praise a big business man personally, as men used to praise a king. They not only find political reasons for the commercial schemes —that they have done for some time past—they also find moral defences for the commercial schemers. They describe the capitalist's brain of steel and heart of gold in a way that Englishmen hitherto have been at least in the habit of reserving for romantic figures like Garibaldi or Gordon. In one excellent magazine Mr. T. P. O'Connor, who, when he likes, can write on letters like a man of letters, has some purple pages of praise of Sir Joseph Lyons—the man who runs those teashop places.

He incidentally brought in a delightful passage about the beautiful souls possessed by some people called Salmon and Gluckstein. I think I like best the passage where he said that Lyons's charming social accomplishments included a talent for "imitating a Jew." The article is accompanied with a large and somewhat leering portrait of that shopkeeper, which makes the parlour-trick in question particularly astonishing. Another literary man, who certainly ought to know better, wrote in another paper a piece of hero-worship about Mr. Selfridge. No doubt the fashion will spread, and the art of words, as polished and pointed by Ruskin or Meredith, will be perfected yet further to explore the labyrinthine heart of Harrod; or compare the simple stoicism of Marshall with the saintly charm of Snelgrove.

Any man can be praised—and rightly praised. If he only stands on two legs he does something a cow cannot do. If a rich man can manage to stand on two legs for a reasonable time, it is called self-control. If he has only one leg, it is called (with some truth) self-sacrifice. I could say something nice (and true) about every man I have ever met. Therefore, I do not doubt I could find something nice about Lyons or Selfridge if I searched for it. But I shall not. The nearest postman or cab-man will provide me with just the same brain of steel and heart of gold as these unlucky lucky men. But I do resent the whole age of patronage being revived under such absurd patrons; and all poets becoming court poets, under kings that have taken no oath, nor led us into any battle.

III. Unbusinesslike Business

The fairy tales we were all taught did not, like the history we were all taught, consist entirely of lies. Parts of the tale of "Puss in Boots" or "Jack and the Beanstalk" may strike the realistic eye as a little unlikely and out of the common way, so to speak; but they contain some very solid and very practical truths. For instance, it may be noted that both in "Puss in Boots" and "Jack and the Beanstalk" if I remember aright, the ogre was not only an ogre but also a magician. And it will generally be found that in all such popular narratives, the king, if he is a wicked king, is generally also a wizard. Now there is a very vital human truth enshrined in this. Bad government, like good government, is a spiritual thing. Even the tyrant never rules by force alone; but mostly by fairy tales. And so it is with the modern tyrant, the great employer. The sight of a millionaire is seldom, in the ordinary sense, an enchanting sight: nevertheless, he is in his way an enchanter. As they say in the gushing articles about him in the magazines, he is a fascinating personality. So is a snake. At least he is fascinating to rabbits; and so is the millionaire to the rabbit-witted sort of people that ladies and gentlemen have allowed themselves to become. He does, in a manner, cast a spell, such as that which imprisoned princes and princesses under the shapes of falcons or stags. He has truly turned men into sheep, as Circe turned them into swine.

Now, the chief of the fairy tales, by which he gains this glory and glamour, is a certain hazy association he has managed to create between the idea of bigness and the idea of practicality. Numbers of the rabbit-witted ladies and gentlemen do really think, in spite of themselves and their experience, that so long as a shop has hundreds of different doors and a great many hot and unhealthy underground departments (they must be hot; this is very important), and more people than would be needed for a man-of-war, or crowded cathedral, to say: "This way, madam," and "The next article, sir," it follows that the goods are good. In short, they hold that the big businesses are businesslike. They are not. Any housekeeper in a truthful mood, that is to say, any housekeeper in a bad temper, will tell you that they are not. But housekeepers, too, are human, and therefore inconsistent and complex; and they do not always stick to truth and bad temper. They are also affected by this queer idolatry of the enormous and elaborate; and cannot help feeling that anything so complicated must go like clockwork. But complexity is no guarantee of accuracy—in clockwork or in anything else. A clock can be as wrong as the human head; and a clock can stop, as suddenly as the human heart. But this strange poetry of plutocracy prevails over people against their very senses. You write to one of the great London stores or emporia, asking, let us say, for an umbrella. A month or two afterwards you receive a very elaborately constructed parcel, containing a broken parasol. You are very pleased. You are gratified to reflect on what a vast number of assistants and employees had combined to break that parasol. You luxuriate in the memory of all those long rooms and departments and wonder in which of them the parasol that you never ordered was broken. Or you want a toy elephant for your child on Christmas Day; as children, like all nice and healthy people, are very ritualistic. Some week or so after Twelfth Night, let us say, you have the pleasure of removing three layers of pasteboards, five layers of brown paper, and fifteen layers of tissue paper and discovering the fragments of an artificial crocodile. You smile in an expansive spirit. You feel that your soul has been broadened by the vision of incompetence conducted on so large a scale. You admire all the more the colossal and Omnipresent Brain of the Organiser of Industry, who amid all his multitudinous cares did not disdain to remember his duty of smashing even the smallest toy of the smallest child. Or, supposing you have asked him to send you some two rolls of cocoa-nut matting: and supposing (after a due interval for reflection) he duly delivers to you the five rolls of wire netting. You take pleasure in the consideration of a mystery: which coarse minds might have called a mistake. It consoles you to know how big the business is: and what an enormous number of people were needed to make such a mistake.

That is the romance that has been told about the big shops; in the literature and art which they have bought, and which (as I said in my recent articles) will soon be quite indistinguishable from their ordinary advertisements. The literature is commercial; and it is only fair to say that the commerce is often really literary. It is no romance, but only rubbish.

The big commercial concerns of to-day are quite exceptionally incompetent. They will be even more incompetent when they are omnipotent. Indeed, that is, and always has been, the whole point of a monopoly; the old and sound argument against a monopoly. It is only because it is incompetent that it has to be omnipotent. When one large shop occupies the whole of one side of a street (or sometimes both sides), it does so in order that men may be unable to get what they want; and may be forced to buy what they don't want. That the rapidly approaching kingdom of the Capitalists will ruin art and letters, I have already said. I say here that in the only sense that can be called human, it will ruin trade, too.

I will not let Christmas go by, even when writing for a revolutionary paper necessarily appealing to many with none of my religious sympathies, without appealing to those sympathies. I knew a man who sent to a great rich shop for a figure for a group of Bethlehem. It arrived broken. I think that is exactly all that business men have now the sense to do.

IV. The War on Holidays

The general proposition, not always easy to define exhaustively, that the reign of the capitalist will be the reign of the cad—that is, of the unlicked type that is neither the citizen nor the gentleman—can be excellently studied in its attitude towards holidays. The special emblematic Employer of to-day, especially the Model Employer (who is the worst sort) has in his starved and evil heart a sincere hatred of holidays. I do not mean that he necessarily wants all his workmen to work until they drop; that only occurs when he happens to be stupid as well as wicked. I do not mean to say that he is necessarily unwilling to grant what he would call "decent hours of labour." He may treat men like dirt; but if you want to make money, even out of dirt, you must let it lie fallow by some rotation of rest. He may treat men as dogs, but unless he is a lunatic he will for certain periods let sleeping dogs lie.

But humane and reasonable hours for labour have nothing whatever to do with the idea of holidays. It is not even a question of ten hours day and eight-hours day; it is not a question of cutting down leisure to the space necessary for food, sleep and exercise. If the modern employer came to the conclusion, for some reason or other, that he could get most out of his men by working them hard for only two hours a day, his whole mental attitude would still be foreign and hostile to holidays. For his whole mental attitude is that the passive time and the active time are alike useful for him and his business. All is, indeed, grist that comes to his mill, including the millers. His slaves still serve him in unconsciousness, as dogs still hunt in slumber. His grist is ground not only by the sounding wheels of iron, but by the soundless wheel of blood and brain. His sacks are still filling silently when the doors are shut on the streets and the sound of the grinding is low.

The Great Holiday

Now a holiday has no connection with using a man either by beating or feeding him. When you give a man a holiday you give him back his body and soul. It is quite possible you may be doing him an injury (though he seldom thinks so), but that does not affect the question for those to whom a holiday is holy. Immortality is the great holiday; and a holiday, like the immortality in the old theologies, is a double-edged privilege. But wherever it is genuine it is simply the restoration and completion of the man. If people ever looked at the printed word under their eye, the word "recreation" would be like the word "resurrection," the blast of a trumpet.

A man, being merely useful, is necessarily incomplete, especially if he be a modern man and means by being useful being "utilitarian." A man going into a modern club gives up his hat; a man going into a modern factory gives up his head. He then goes in and works loyally for the old firm to build up the great fabric of commerce (which can be done without a head), but when he has done work he goes to the cloak-room, like the man at the club, and gets his head back again; that is the germ of the holiday. It may be urged that the club man who leaves his hat often goes away with another hat; and perhaps it may be the same with the factory hand who has left his head. A hand that has lost its head may affect the fastidious as a mixed metaphor; but, God pardon us all, what an unmixed truth! We could almost prove the whole ease from the habit of calling human beings merely "hands" while they are working; as if the hand were horribly cut off, like the hand that has offended; as if, while the sinner entered heaven maimed, his unhappy hand still laboured laying up riches for the lords of hell. But to return to the man whom we found waiting for his head in the cloak-room. It may be urged, we say, that he might take the wrong head, like the wrong hat; but here the similarity ceases. For it has been observed by benevolent onlookers at life's drama that the hat taken away by mistake is frequently better than the real hat; whereas the head taken away after the hours of toil is certainly worse: stained with the cobwebs and dust of this dustbin of all the centuries.

The Supreme Adventure

All the words dedicated to places of eating and drinking are pure and poetic words. Even the word "hotel" is the word hospital. And St. Julien, whose claret I drank this Christmas, was the patron saint of innkeepers, because (as far as I can make out) he was hospitable to lepers. Now I do not say that the ordinary hotel-keeper in Piccadilly or the Avenue de l'Opera would embrace a leper, slap him on the back, and ask him to order what he liked; but I do say that hospitality is his trade virtue. And I do also say it is well to keep before our eyes the supreme adventure of a virtue. If you are brave, think of the man who was braver than you. If you are kind, think of the man who was kinder than you.

That is what was meant by having a patron saint. That is the link between the poor saint who received bodily lepers and the great hotel proprietor who (as a rule) receives spiritual lepers. But a word yet weaker than "hotel" illustrates the same point—the word "restaurant." There again you have the admission that there is a definite building or statue to "restore"; that ineffaceable image of man that some call the image of God. And that is the holiday; it is the restaurant or restoring thing that, by a blast of magic, turns a man into himself.

This complete and reconstructed man is the nightmare of the modern capitalist. His whole scheme would crack across like a mirror of Shallot, if once a plain man were ready for his two plain duties—ready to live and ready to die. And that horror of holidays which marks the modern capitalist is very largely a horror of the vision of a whole human being: something that is not a "hand" or a "head for figures." But an awful creature who has met himself in the wilderness. The employers will give time to eat, time to sleep; they are in terror of a time to think.

To anyone who knows any history it is wholly needless to say that holidays have been destroyed. As Mr. Belloc, who knows much more history than you or I, recently pointed out in the "Pall Mall Magazine," Shakespeare's title of "Twelfth Night: or What You Will" simply meant that a winter carnival for everybody went on wildly till the twelfth night after Christmas. Those of my readers who work for modern offices or factories might ask their employers for twelve days' holidays after Christmas. And they might let me know the reply.

V. THE CHURCH OF THE SERVILE STATE

I confess I cannot see why mere blasphemy by itself should be an excuse for tyranny and treason; or how the mere isolated fact of a man not believing in God should be a reason for my believing in Him.

But the rather spinsterish flutter among some of the old Freethinkers has put one tiny ripple of truth in it; and that affects the idea which I wish to emphasise even to monotony in these pages. I mean the idea that the new community which the capitalists are now constructing will be a very complete and absolute community; and one which will tolerate nothing really independent of itself. Now, it is true that any positive creed, true or false, would tend to be independent of itself. It might be Roman Catholicism or Mahomedanism or Materialism; but, if strongly held, it would be a thorn in the side of the Servile State. The Moslem thinks all men immortal: the Materialist thinks all men mortal. But the Moslem does not think the rich Sinbad will live forever; but the poor Sinbad will die on his deathbed. The Materialist does not think that Mr. Haeckel will go to heaven, while all the peasants will go to pot, like their chickens. In every serious doctrine of the destiny of men, there is some trace of the doctrine of the equality of men. But the capitalist really depends on some religion of inequality. The capitalist must somehow distinguish himself from human kind; he must be obviously above it—or he would be obviously below it. Take even the least attractive and popular side of the larger religions to-day; take the mere vetoes imposed by Islam on Atheism or Catholicism. The Moslem veto upon intoxicants cuts across all classes. But it is absolutely necessary for the capitalist (who presides at a Licensing Committee, and also at a large dinner), it is absolutely necessary for him, to make a distinction between gin and champagne. The Atheist veto upon all miracles cuts across all classes. But it is absolutely necessary for the capitalist to make a distinction between his wife (who is an aristocrat and consults crystal gazers and star gazers in the West End), and vulgar miracles claimed by gipsies or travelling showmen. The Catholic veto upon usury, as defined in dogmatic councils, cuts across all classes. But it is absolutely necessary to the capitalist to distinguish more delicately between two kinds of usury; the kind he finds useful and the kind he does not find useful. The religion of the Servile State must have no dogmas or definitions. It cannot afford to have any definitions. For definitions are very dreadful things: they do the two things that most men, especially comfortable men, cannot endure. They fight; and they fight fair.

Every religion, apart from open devil worship, must appeal to a virtue or the pretence of a virtue. But a virtue, generally speaking, does some good to everybody. It is therefore necessary to distinguish among the people it was meant to benefit those whom it does benefit. Modern broad-mindedness benefits the rich; and benefits nobody else. It was meant to benefit the rich; and meant to benefit nobody else. And if you think this unwarranted, I will put before you one plain question. There are some pleasures of the poor that may also mean profits for the rich: there are other pleasures of the poor which cannot mean profits for the rich? Watch this one contrast, and you will watch the whole creation of a careful slavery.

In the last resort the two things called Beer and Soap end only in a froth. They are both below the high notice of a real religion. But there is just this difference: that the soap makes the factory more satisfactory, while the beer only makes the workman more satisfied. Wait and see if the Soap does not increase and the Beer decrease. Wait and see whether the religion of the Servile State is not in every case what I say: the encouragement of small virtues supporting capitalism, the discouragement of the huge virtues that defy it. Many great religions, Pagan and Christian, have insisted on wine. Only one, I think, has insisted on Soap. You will find it in the New Testament attributed to the Pharisees.

VI. SCIENCE AND THE EUGENISTS

The key fact in the new development of plutocracy is that it will use its own blunder as an excuse for further crimes. Everywhere the very completeness of the impoverishment will be made a reason for the enslavement; though the men who impoverished were the same who enslaved. It is as if a highwayman not only took away a gentleman's horse and all his money, but then handed him over to the police for tramping without visible means of subsistence. And the most monstrous feature in this enormous meanness may be noted in the plutocratic appeal to science, or, rather, to the pseudo-science that they call Eugenics.

The Eugenists get the ear of the humane but rather hazy cliques by saying that the present "conditions" under which people work and breed are bad for the race; but the modern mind will not generally stretch beyond one step of reasoning, and the consequence which appears to follow on the consideration of these "conditions" is by no means what would originally have been expected. If somebody says: "A rickety cradle may mean a rickety baby," the natural deduction, one would think, would be to give the people a good cradle, or give them money enough to buy one. But that means higher wages and greater equalisation of wealth; and the plutocratic scientist, with a slightly troubled expression, turns his eyes and pince-nez in another direction.

Reduced to brutal terms of truth, his difficulty is this and simply this: More food, leisure, and money for the workman would mean a better workman, better even from the point of view of anyone for whom he worked. But more food, leisure, and money would also mean a more independent workman. A house with a decent fire and a full pantry would be a better house to make a chair or mend a clock in, even from the customer's point of view, than a hovel with a leaky roof and a cold hearth. But a house with a decent fire and a full pantry would also be a better house in which to refuse to make a chair or mend a clock—a much better house to do nothing in—and doing nothing is sometimes one of the highest of the duties of man. All but the hard-hearted must be torn with pity for this pathetic dilemma of the rich man, who has to keep the poor man just stout enough to do the work and just thin enough to have to do it. As he stood gazing at the leaky roof and the rickety cradle in a pensive manner, there one day came into his mind a new and curious idea—one of the most strange, simple, and horrible ideas that have ever risen from the deep pit of original sin.

The roof could not be mended, or, at least, it could not be mended much, without upsetting the capitalist balance, or, rather, disproportion in society; for a man with a roof is a man with a house, and to that extent his house is his castle. The cradle could not be made to rock easier, or, at least, not much easier, without strengthening the hands of the poor household, for the hand that rocks the cradle rules the world—to that extent. But it occurred to the capitalist that there was one sort of furniture in the house that could be altered. The husband and wife could be altered. Birth costs nothing, except in pain and valour and such old-fashioned things; and the merchant need pay no more for mating a strong miner to a healthy fishwife than he pays when the miner mates himself with a less robust female whom he has the sentimentality to prefer. Thus it might be possible, by keeping on certain broad lines of heredity, to have some physical improvement without any moral, political, or social improvement. It might be possible to keep a supply of strong and healthy slaves without coddling them with decent conditions. As the mill-owners use the wind and the water to drive their mills, they would use this natural force as something even cheaper; and turn their wheels by diverting from its channel the blood of a man in his youth. That is what Eugenics means; and that is all that it means.

Of the moral state of those who think of such things it does not become us to speak. The practical question is rather the intellectual one: of whether their calculations are well founded, and whether the men of science can or will guarantee them any such physical certainties. Fortunately, it becomes clearer every day that they are, scientifically speaking, building on the shifting sand. The theory of breeding slaves breaks down through what a democrat calls the equality of men, but which even an oligarchist will find himself forced to call the similarity of men. That is, that though it is not true that all men are normal, it is overwhelmingly certain that most men are normal. All the common Eugenic arguments are drawn from extreme cases, which, even if human honour and laughter allowed of their being eliminated, would not by their elimination greatly affect the mass. For the rest, there remains the enormous weakness in Eugenics, that if ordinary men's judgment or liberty is to be discounted in relation to heredity, the judgment of the judges must be discounted in relation to their heredity. The Eugenic professor may or may not succeed in choosing a baby's parents; it is quite certain that he cannot succeed in choosing his own parents. All his thoughts, including his Eugenic thoughts, are, by the very principle of those thoughts, flowing from a doubtful or tainted source. In short, we should need a perfectly Wise Man to do the thing at all. And if he were a Wise Man he would not do it.

VII. THE EVOLUTION OF THE PRISON

I have never understood why it is that those who talk most about evolution, and talk it in the very age of fashionable evolutionism, do not see the one way in which evolution really does apply to our modern difficulty. There is, of course, an element of evolutionism in the universe; and I know no religion or philosophy that ever entirely ignored it. Evolution, popularly speaking, is that which happens to unconscious things. They grow unconsciously; or fade unconsciously; or rather, some parts of them grow and some parts of them fade; and at any given moment there is almost always some presence of the fading thing, and some incompleteness in the growing one. Thus, if I went to sleep for a hundred years, like the Sleeping Beauty (I wish I could), I should grow a beard—unlike the Sleeping Beauty. And just as I should grow hair if I were asleep, I should grow grass if I were dead. Those whose religion it was that God was asleep were perpetually impressed and affected by the fact that he had a long beard. And those whose philosophy it is that the universe is dead from the beginning (being the grave of nobody in particular) think that is the way that grass can grow. In any case, these developments only occur with dead or dreaming things. What happens when everyone is asleep is called Evolution. What happens when everyone is awake is called Revolution.

There was once an honest man, whose name I never knew, but whose face I can almost see (it is framed in Victorian whiskers and fixed in a Victorian neck-cloth), who was balancing the achievements of France and England in civilisation and social efficiencies. And when he came to the religious aspect he said that there were more stone and brick churches used in France; but, on the other hand, there are more sects in England. Whether such a lively disintegration is a proof of vitality in any valuable sense I have always doubted. The sun may breed maggots in a dead dog; but it is essential for such a liberation of life that the dog should be unconscious or (to say the least of it) absent-minded. Broadly speaking, you may call the thing corruption, if you happen to like dogs. You may call it evolution, if you happen to like maggots. In either case, it is what happens to things if you leave them alone.

The Evolutionists' Error

Now, the modern Evolutionists have made no real use of the idea of evolution, especially in the matter of social prediction. They always fall into what is (from their logical point of view) the error of supposing that evolution knows what it is doing. They predict the State of the future as a fruit rounded and polished. But the whole point of evolution (the only point there is in it) is that no State will ever be rounded and polished, because it will always contain some organs that outlived their use, and some that have not yet fully found theirs. If we wish to prophesy what will happen, we must imagine things now moderate grown enormous; things now local grown universal; things now promising grown triumphant; primroses bigger than sunflowers, and sparrows stalking about like flamingoes.

In other words, we must ask what modern institution has a future before it? What modern institution may have swollen to six times its present size in the social heat and growth of the future? I do not think the Garden City will grow: but of that I may speak in my next and last article of this series. I do not think even the ordinary Elementary School, with its compulsory education, will grow. Too many unlettered people hate the teacher for teaching; and too many lettered people hate the teacher for not teaching. The Garden City will not bear much blossom; the young idea will not shoot, unless it shoots the teacher. But the one flowering tree on the estate, the one natural expansion which I think will expand, is the institution we call the Prison.

Prisons for All

If the capitalists are allowed to erect their constructive capitalist community, I speak quite seriously when I say that I think Prison will become an almost universal experience. It will not necessarily be a cruel or shameful experience: on these points (I concede certainly for the present purpose of debate) it may be a vastly improved experience. The conditions in the prison, very possibly, will be made more humane. But the prison will be made more humane only in order to contain more of humanity. I think little of the judgment and sense of humour of any man who can have watched recent police trials without realising that it is no longer a question of whether the law has been broken by a crime; but, now, solely a question of whether the situation could be mended by an imprisonment. It was so with Tom Mann; it was so with Larkin; it was so with the poor atheist who was kept in gaol for saying something he had been acquitted of saying: it is so in such cases day by day. We no longer lock a man up for doing something; we lock him up in the hope of his doing nothing. Given this principle, it is evidently possible to make the mere conditions of punishment more moderate, or—(more probably) more secret. There may really be more mercy in the Prison, on condition that there is less justice in the Court. I should not be surprised if, before we are done with all this, a man was allowed to smoke in prison, on condition, of course, that he had been put in prison for smoking.

Now that is the process which, in the absence of democratic protest, will certainly proceed, will increase and multiply and replenish the earth and subdue it. Prison may even lose its disgrace for a little time: it will be difficult to make it disgraceful when men like Larkin can be imprisoned for no reason at all, just as his celebrated ancestor was hanged for no reason at all. But capitalist society, which naturally does not know the meaning of honour, cannot know the meaning of disgrace: and it will still go on imprisoning for no reason at all. Or rather for that rather simple reason that makes a cat spring or a rat run away.

It matters little whether our masters stoop to state the matter in the form that every prison should be a school; or in the more candid form that every school should be a prison. They have already fulfilled their servile principle in the case of the schools. Everyone goes to the Elementary Schools except the few people who tell them to go there. I prophesy that (unless our revolt succeeds) nearly everyone will be going to Prison, with a precisely similar patience.

VIII. THE LASH FOR LABOUR

If I were to prophesy that two hundred years hence a grocer would have the right and habit of beating the grocer's assistant with a stick, or that shop girls might be flogged, as they already can be fined, many would regard it as rather a rash remark. It would be a rash remark. Prophecy is always unreliable; unless we except the kind which is avowedly irrational, mystical and supernatural prophecy. But relatively to nearly all the other prophecies that are being made around me to-day, I should say my prediction stood an exceptionally good chance. In short, I think the grocer with the stick is a figure we are far more likely to see than the Superman or the Samurai, or the True Model Employer, or the Perfect Fabian Official, or the citizen of the Collectivist State. And it is best for us to see the full ugliness of the transformation which is passing over our Society in some such abrupt and even grotesque image at the end of it. The beginnings of a decline, in every age of history, have always had the appearance of being reforms. Nero not only fiddled while Rome was burning, but he probably really paid more attention to the fiddle than to the fire. The Roi Soleil, like many other soleils, was most splendid to all appearance a little before sunset. And if I ask myself what will be the ultimate and final fruit of all our social reforms, garden cities, model employers, insurances, exchanges, arbitration courts, and so on, then, I say, quite seriously, "I think it will be labour under the lash."

The Sultan and the Sack

Let us arrange in some order a number of converging considerations that all point in this direction. (1) It is broadly true, no doubt, that the weapon of the employer has hitherto been the threat of dismissal, that is, the threat of enforced starvation. He is a Sultan who need not order the bastinado, so long as he can order the sack. But there are not a few signs that this weapon is not quite so convenient and flexible a one as his increasing rapacities require. The fact of the introduction of fines, secretly or openly, in many shops and factories, proves that it is convenient for the capitalists to have some temporary and adjustable form of punishment besides the final punishment of pure ruin. Nor is it difficult to see the commonsense of this from their wholly inhuman point of view. The act of sacking a man is attended with the same disadvantages as the act of shooting a man: one of which is that you can get no more out of him. It is, I am told, distinctly annoying to blow a fellow creature's brains out with a revolver and then suddenly remember that he was the only person who knew where to get the best Russian cigarettes. So our Sultan, who is the orderer of the sack, is also the bearer of the bow-string. A school in which there was no punishment, except expulsion, would be a school in which it would be very difficult to keep proper discipline; and the sort of discipline on which the reformed capitalism will insist will be all of the type which in free nations is imposed only on children. Such a school would probably be in a chronic condition of breaking up for the holidays. And the reasons for the insufficiency of this extreme instrument are also varied and evident. The materialistic Sociologists, who talk about the survival of the fittest and the weakest going to the wall (and whose way of looking at the world is to put on the latest and most powerful scientific spectacles, and then shut their eyes), frequently talk as if a workman were simply efficient or non-efficient, as if a criminal were reclaimable or irreclaimable. The employers have sense enough at least to know better than that. They can see that a servant may be useful in one way and exasperating in another; that he may be bad in one part of his work and good in another; that he may be occasionally drunk and yet generally indispensable. Just as a practical school-master would know that a schoolboy can be at once the plague and the pride of the school. Under these circumstances small and varying penalties are obviously the most convenient things for the person keeping order; an underling can be punished for coming late, and yet do useful work when he comes. It will be possible to give a rap over the knuckles without wholly cutting off the right hand that has offended. Under these circumstances the employers have naturally resorted to fines. But there is a further ground for believing that the process will go beyond fines before it is completed.

(2) The fine is based on the old European idea that everybody possesses private property in some reasonable degree; but not only is this not true to-day, but it is not being made any truer, even by those who honestly believe that they are mending matters. The great employers will often do something towards improving what they call the "conditions" of their workers; but a worker might have his conditions as carefully arranged as a racehorse has, and still have no more personal property than a racehorse. If you take an average poor seamstress or factory girl, you will find that the power of chastising her through her property has very considerable limits; it is almost as hard for the employer of labour to tax her for punishment as it is for the Chancellor of the Exchequer to tax her for revenue. The next most obvious thing to think of, of course, would be imprisonment, and that might be effective enough under simpler conditions. An old-fashioned shopkeeper might have locked up his apprentice in his coal-cellar; but his coal-cellar would be a real, pitch dark coal-cellar, and the rest of his house would be a real human house. Everybody (especially the apprentice) would see a most perceptible difference between the two. But, as I pointed out in the article before this, the whole tendency of the capitalist legislation and experiment is to make imprisonment much more general and automatic, while making it, or professing to make it, more humane. In other words, the hygienic prison and the servile factory will become so uncommonly like each other that the poor man will hardly know or care whether he is at the moment expiating an offence or merely swelling a dividend. In both places there will be the same sort of shiny tiles. In neither place will there be any cell so unwholesome as a coal-cellar or so wholesome as a home. The weapon of the prison, therefore, like the weapon of the fine, will be found to have considerable limitations to its effectiveness when employed against the wretched reduced citizen of our day. Whether it be property or liberty you cannot take from him what he has not got. You cannot imprison a slave, because you cannot enslave a slave.

(3) Most people, on hearing the suggestion that it may come to corporal punishment at last (as it did in every slave system I ever heard of, including some that were generally kindly, and even successful), will merely be struck with horror and incredulity, and feel that such a barbarous revival is unthinkable in the modern atmosphere. How far it will be, or need be, a revival of the actual images and methods of ruder times I will discuss in a moment. But first, as another of the converging lines tending to corporal punishment, consider this: that for some reason or other the old full-blooded and masculine humanitarianism in this matter has weakened and fallen silent; it has weakened and fallen silent in a very curious manner, the precise reason for which I do not altogether understand. I knew the average Liberal, the average Nonconformist minister, the average Labour Member, the average middle-class Socialist, were, with all their good qualities, very deficient in what I consider a respect for the human soul. But I did imagine that they had the ordinary modern respect for the human body. The fact, however, is clear and incontrovertible. In spite of the horror of all humane people, in spite of the hesitation even of our corrupt and panic-stricken Parliament, measures can now be triumphantly passed for spreading or increasing the use of physical torture, and for applying it to the newest and vaguest categories of crime. Thirty or forty years ago, nay, twenty years ago, when Mr. F. Hugh O'Donnell and others forced a Liberal Government to drop the cat-o-nine-tails like a scorpion, we could have counted on a mass of honest hatred of such things. We cannot count on it now.

(4) But lastly, it is not necessary that in the factories of the future the institution of physical punishment should actually remind people of the jambok or the knout. It could easily be developed out of the many forms of physical discipline which are already used by employers on the excuses of education or hygiene. Already in some factories girls are obliged to swim whether they like it or not, or do gymnastics whether they like it or not. By a simple extension of hours

or complication of exercises a pair of Swedish clubs could easily be so used as to leave their victim as exhausted as one who had come off the rack. I think it extremely likely that they will be.

IX. THE MASK OF SOCIALISM

The chief aim of all honest Socialists just now is to prevent the coming of Socialism. I do not say it as a sneer, but, on the contrary, as a compliment; a compliment to their political instinct and public spirit. I admit it may be called an exaggeration; but there really is a sort of sham Socialism that the modern politicians may quite possibly agree to set up; if they do succeed in setting it up, the battle for the poor is lost.

We must note, first of all, a general truth about the curious time we live in. It will not be so difficult as some people may suppose to make the Servile State look rather like Socialism, especially to the more pedantic kind of Socialist. The reason is this. The old lucid and trenchant expounder of Socialism, such as Blatchford or Fred Henderson, always describes the economic power of the plutocrats as consisting in private property. Of course, in a sense, this is quite true; though they too often miss the point that private property, as such, is not the same as property confined to the few. But the truth is that the situation has grown much more subtle; perhaps too subtle, not to say too insane, for straight-thinking theorists like Blatchford. The rich man to-day does not only rule by using private property; he also rules by treating public property as if it were private property. A man like Lord Murray pulled the strings, especially the purse-strings; but the whole point of his position was that all sorts of strings had got entangled. The secret strength of the money he held did not lie merely in the fact that it was his money. It lay precisely in the fact that nobody had any clear idea of whether it was his money, or his successor's money, or his brother's money, or the Marconi Company's money, or the Liberal Party's money, or the English Nation's money. It was buried treasure; but it was not private property. It was the acme of plutocracy because it was not private property. Now, by following this precedent, this unprincipled vagueness about official and unofficial moneys by the cheerful habit of always mixing up the money in the pocket with the money in the till, it would be quite possible to keep the rich as rich as ever in practice, though they might have suffered confiscation in theory. Mr. Lloyd George has four hundred a year as an M. P.; but he not only gets much more as a Minister, but he might at any time get immeasurably more by speculating on State secrets that are necessarily known to him. Some say that he has even attempted something of the kind. Now, it would be quite possible to cut Mr. George down, not to four hundred a year, but to fourpence a day; and still leave him all these other and enormous financial superiorities. It must be remembered that a Socialist State, in any way resembling a modern State, must, however egalitarian it may be, have the handling of huge sums, and the enjoyment of large conveniences; it is not improbable that the same men will handle and enjoy in much the same manner, though in theory they are doing it as instruments, and not as individuals. For instance, the Prime Minister has a private house, which is also (I grieve to inform that eminent Puritan) a public house. It is supposed to be a sort of Government office; though people do not generally give children's parties, or go to bed in a Government office. I do not know where Mr. Herbert Samuel lives; but I have no doubt he does himself well in the matter of decoration and furniture. On the existing official parallel there is no need to move any of these things in order to Socialise them. There is no need to withdraw one diamond-headed nail from the carpet; or one golden teaspoon from the tray. It is only necessary to call it an official residence, like 10 Downing-street. I think it is not at all improbable that this Plutocracy, pretending to be a Bureaucracy, will be attempted or achieved. Our wealthy rulers will be in the position which grumblers in the world of sport sometimes attribute to some of the "gentlemen" players. They assert that some of these are paid like any professional; only their pay is called their expenses. This system might run side by side with a theory of equal wages, as absolute as that once laid down by Mr. Bernard Shaw. By the theory of the State, Mr. Herbert

Samuel and Mr. Lloyd George might be humble citizens, drudging for their fourpence a day; and no better off than porters and coal-heavers. If there were presented to our mere senses what appeared to be the form of Mr. Herbert Samuel in an astrakhan coat and a motor-car, we should find the record of the expenditure (if we could find it at all) under the heading of "Speed Limit Extension Enquiry Commission." If it fell to our lot to behold (with the eye of flesh) what seemed to be Mr. Lloyd George lying in a hammock and smoking a costly cigar, we should know that the expenditure would be divided between the "Condition of Rope and Netting Investigation Department," and the "State of Cuban Tobacco Trade: Imperial Inspector's Report."

Such is the society I think they will build unless we can knock it down as fast as they build it. Everything in it, tolerable or intolerable, will have but one use; and that use what our ancestors used to call usance or usury. Its art may be good or bad, but it will be an advertisement for usurers; its literature may be good or bad, but it will appeal to the patronage of usurers; its scientific selection will select according to the needs of usurers; its religion will be just charitable enough to pardon usurers; its penal system will be just cruel enough to crush all the critics of usurers: the truth of it will be Slavery: and the title of it may quite possibly be Socialism.

THE ESCAPE

We watched you building, stone by stone,
The well-washed cells and well-washed graves
We shall inhabit but not own
When Britons ever shall be slaves;
The water's waiting in the trough,
The tame oats sown are portioned free,
There is Enough, and just Enough,
And all is ready now but we.
But you have not caught us yet, my lords,
You have us still to get.
A sorry army you'd have got,
Its flags are rags that float and rot,
Its drums are empty pan and pot,
Its baggage is—an empty cot;
But you have not caught us yet.
A little; and we might have slipped
When came your rumours and your sales
And the foiled rich men, feeble-lipped,
Said and unsaid their sorry tales;
Great God! It needs a bolder brow
To keep ten sheep inside a pen,
And we are sheep no longer now;
You are but Masters. We are Men.
We give you all good thanks, my lords,
We buy at easy price;

Thanks for the thousands that you stole,
The bribes by wire, the bets on coal,
The knowledge of that naked whole
That hath delivered our flesh and soul
Out of your Paradise.
We had held safe your parks; but when
Men taunted you with bribe and fee,
We only saw the Lord of Men
Grin like an Ape and climb a tree;
And humbly had we stood without
Your princely barns; did we not see
In pointed faces peering out
What Rats now own the granary.
It is too late, too late, my lords,
We give you back your grace:
You cannot with all cajoling
Make the wet ditch, or winds that sting,
Lost pride, or the pawned wedding rings,
Or drink or Death a blacker thing
Than a smile upon your face.

THE NEW RAID

The two kinds of social reform, one of which might conceivably free us at last while the other would certainly enslave us forever, are exhibited in an easy working model in the two efforts that have been made for the soldiers' wives—I mean the effort to increase their allowance and the effort to curtail their alleged drinking. In the preliminary consideration, at any rate, we must see the second question as quite detached from our own sympathies on the special subject of fermented liquor. It could be applied to any other pleasure or ornament of life; it will be applied to every other pleasure and ornament of life if the Capitalist campaign can succeed. The argument we know; but it cannot be too often made clear. An employer, let us say, pays a seamstress twopence a day, and she does not seem to thrive on it. So little, perhaps, does she thrive on it that the employer has even some difficulty in thriving upon her. There are only two things that he can do, and the distinction between them cuts the whole social and political world in two. It is a touchstone by which we can—not sometimes, but always—distinguish economic equality from servile social reform. He can give the girl some magnificent sum, such as sixpence a day, to do as she likes with, and trust that her improved health and temper will work for the benefit of his business. Or he may keep her to the original sum of a shilling a week, but earmark each of the pennies to be used or not to be used for a particular purpose. If she must not spend this penny on a bunch of violets, or that penny on a novelette, or the other penny on a toy for some baby, it is possible that she will concentrate her expenditure more upon physical necessities, and so become, from the employer's point of view, a more efficient person. Without the trouble of adding twopence to her wages, he has added twopenny-worth to her food. In short, she has the holy satisfaction of being worth more without being paid more.

This Capitalist is an ingenious person, and has many polished characteristics; but I think the most singular thing about him is his staggering lack of shame. Neither the hour of death nor the day of reckoning, neither the tent of exile nor the house of mourning, neither chivalry nor patriotism, neither womanhood nor widowhood, is safe at this supreme moment from his dirty little expedient of dieting the slave. As similar bullies, when they collect the slum rents, put a foot in the open door, these are always ready to push in a muddy wedge wherever there is a slit in a sundered household or a crack in a broken heart. To a man of any manhood nothing can be conceived more loathsome and sacrilegious than even so much as asking whether a woman who has given up all she loved to death and the fatherland has or has not shown some weakness in her seeking for self-comfort. I know not in which of the two cases I should count myself the baser for inquiring—a case where the charge was false or a case where it was true. But the philanthropic employer of the sort I describe is not a man of any manhood; in a sense he is not a man at all. He shows some consciousness of the fact when he calls his workers "men" as distinct from masters. He cannot comprehend the gallantry of costermongers or the delicacy that is quite common among cabmen. He finds this social reform by half-rations on the whole to his mercantile profit, and it will be hard to get him to think of anything else.

But there are people assisting him, people like the Duchess of Marlborough, who know not their right hand from their left, and to these we may legitimately address our remonstrance and a resume of some of the facts they do not know. The Duchess of Marlborough is, I believe, an American, and this separates her from the problem in a special way, because the drink question in America is entirely different from the drink question in England. But I wish the Duchess of Marlborough would pin up in her private study, side by side with the Declaration of Independence, a document recording the following simple truths: (1) Beer, which is largely drunk in public-houses, is not a spirit or a grog or a cocktail or a drug. It is the common English liquid for quenching the thirst; it is so still among innumerable gentlemen, and, until very lately, was so among innumerable ladies. Most of us remember dames of the last generation whose manners were fit for Versailles, and who drank ale or Stout as a matter of course. Schoolboys drank ale as a matter of course, and their schoolmasters gave it to them as a matter of course. To tell a poor woman that she must not have any until half the day is over is simply cracked, like telling a dog or a child that he must not have water. (2) The public-house is not a secret rendezvous of bad characters. It is the open and obvious place for a certain purpose, which all men used for that purpose until the rich began to be snobs and the poor to become slaves. One might as well warn people against Willesden Junction. (3) Many poor people live in houses where they cannot, without great preparation, offer hospitality. (4) The climate of these picturesque islands does not favour conducting long conversations with one's oldest friends on an iron seat in the park. (5) Halfpast eleven a.m. is not early in the day for a woman who gets up before six. (6) The bodies and minds of these women belong to God and to themselves.

THE NEW NAME

Something has come into our community, which is strong enough to save our community; but which has not yet got a name. Let no one fancy I confess any unreality when I confess the namelessness. The morality called Puritanism, the tendency called Liberalism, the reaction called Tory Democracy, had not only long been powerful, but had practically done most of their work, before these actual names were attached to them. Nevertheless, I think it would be a good thing to have some portable and practicable way of referring to those who think as we do in our main concern. Which is, that men in England are ruled, at this minute by the clock, by brutes who refuse them bread, by liars who refuse them news, and by fools who cannot govern, and therefore wish to enslave.

Let me explain first why I am not satisfied with the word commonly used, which I have often used myself; and which, in some contexts, is quite the right word to use. I mean the word "rebel." Passing over the fact that many who understand the justice of our cause (as a great many at the Universities) would still use the word "rebel" in its old and strict sense as meaning only a disturber of just rule. I pass to a much more practical point. The word "rebel" understates our cause. It is much too mild; it lets our enemies off much too easily. There is a tradition in all western life and letters of Prometheus defying the stars, of man at war with the Universe, and dreaming what nature had never dared to dream. All this is valuable in its place and proportion. But it has nothing whatever to do with our ease; or rather it very much weakens it. The plutocrats will be only too pleased if we profess to preach a new morality; for they know jolly well that they have broken the old one. They will be only too pleased to be able to say that we, by our own confession, are merely restless and negative; that we are only what we call rebels and they call cranks. But it is not true; and we must not concede it to them for a moment. The model millionaire is more of a crank than the Socialists; just as Nero was more of a crank than the Christians. And avarice has gone mad in the governing class to-day, just as lust went mad in the circle of Nero. By all the working and orthodox standards of sanity, capitalism is insane. I should not say to Mr. Rockefeller "I am a rebel." I should say "I am a respectable man: and you are not."

Our Lawless Enemies

But the vital point is that the confession of mere rebellion softens the startling lawlessness of our enemies. Suppose a publisher's clerk politely asked his employer for a rise in his salary; and, on being refused, said he must leave the employment? Suppose the employer knocked him down with a ruler, tied him up as a brown paper parcel, addressed him (in a fine business hand) to the Governor of Rio Janeiro and then asked the policeman to promise never to arrest him for what he had done? That is a precise copy, in every legal and moral principle, of the "deportation of the strikers." They were assaulted and kidnapped for not accepting a contract, and for nothing else; and the act was so avowedly criminal that the law had to be altered afterwards to cover the crime. Now suppose some postal official, between here and Rio Janeiro, had noticed a faint kicking inside the brown paper parcel, and had attempted to ascertain the cause. And suppose the clerk could only explain, in a muffled voice through the brown paper, that he was by constitution and temperament a Rebel. Don't you see that he would be rather understating his case? Don't you see he would be bearing his injuries much too meekly? They might take him out of the parcel; but they would very possibly put him into a mad-house instead. Symbolically speaking, that is what they would like to do with us. Symbolically speaking, the dirty misers who rule us will put us in a mad-house—unless we can put them there.

Or suppose a bank cashier were admittedly allowed to take the money out of the till, and put it loose in his pocket, more or less mixed up with his own money; afterwards laying some of both (at different odds) on "Blue Murder" for the Derby. Suppose when some depositor asked mildly what day the accountants came, he smote that astonished inquirer on the nose, crying: "Slanderer! Mud-slinger!" and suppose he then resigned his position. Suppose no books were shown. Suppose when the new cashier came to be initiated into his duties, the old cashier did not tell him about the money, but confided it to the honour and delicacy of his own maiden aunt at Cricklewood. Suppose he then went off in a yacht to visit the whale fisheries of the North Sea. Well, in every moral and legal principle, that is a precise account of the dealings with the Party Funds. But what would the banker say? What would the clients say? One thing, I think, I can venture to promise; the banker would not march up and down the office exclaiming in rapture, "I'm a rebel! That's what I am, a rebel!" And if he said to the first indignant depositor "You are a rebel," I fear the depositor might answer, "You are a robber." We have no need to elaborate arguments for breaking the law. The capitalists have broken the law. We have no need of further moralities. They have broken their own morality. It is as if you were to run down the street shouting, "Communism! Communism! Share! Share!" after a man who had run away with your watch.

We want a term that will tell everybody that there is, by the common standard, frank fraud and cruelty pushed to their fierce extreme; and that we are fighting THEM. We are not in a state of "divine discontent"; we are in an entirely human and entirely reasonable rage. We say we have been swindled and oppressed, and we are quite ready and able to prove it before any tribunal that allows us to call a swindler a swindler. It is the protection of the present system that most of its tribunals do not. I cannot at the moment think of any party name that would particularly distinguish us from our more powerful and prosperous opponents, unless it were the name the old Jacobites gave themselves; the Honest Party.

Captured Our Standards

I think it is plain that for the purpose of facing these new and infamous modern facts, we cannot, with any safety, depend on any of the old nineteenth century names; Socialist, or Communist, or Radical, or Liberal, or Labour. They are all honourable names; they all stand, or stood, for things in which we may still believe; we can still apply them to other problems; but not to this one. We have no longer a monopoly of these names. Let it be understood that I am not speaking here of the philosophical problem of their meaning, but of the practical problem of their use. When I called myself a Radical I knew Mr. Balfour would not call himself a Radical; therefore there was some use in the word. When I called myself a Socialist I knew Lord Penrhyn would not call himself a Socialist; therefore there was some use in the word. But the capitalists, in that aggressive march which is the main fact of our time, have captured our standards, both in the military and philosophic sense of the word. And it is useless for us to march under colours which they can carry as well as we.

Do you believe in Democracy? The devils also believe and tremble. Do you believe in Trades Unionism? The Labour Members also believe; and tremble like a falling teetotum. Do you believe in the State? The Samuels also believe, and grin. Do you believe in the centralisation of Empire? So did Beit. Do you believe in the decentralisation of Empire? So does Albu. Do you believe in the brotherhood of men: and do you, dear brethren, believe that Brother Arthur Henderson does not? Do you cry, "The world for the workers!" and do you imagine Philip Snowden would not? What we need is a name that shall declare, not that the modern treason and tyranny are bad, but that they are quite literally, intolerable: and that we mean to act accordingly. I really think "the Limits" would be as good a name as any. But, anyhow, something is born among us that is as strong as an infant Hercules: and it is part of my prejudices to want it christened. I advertise for godfathers and godmothers.

A WORKMAN'S HISTORY OF ENGLAND

A thing which does not exist and which is very much wanted is "A Working-Man's History of England." I do not mean a history written for working men (there are whole dustbins of them), I mean a history, written by working men or from the working men's standpoint. I wish five generations of a fisher's or a miner's family could incarnate themselves in one man and tell the story.

It is impossible to ignore altogether any comment coming from so eminent a literary artist as Mr. Laurence Housman, but I do not deal here so specially with his well known conviction about Votes for Women, as with another idea which is, I think, rather at the back of it, if not with him at least with others; and which concerns this matter of the true story of England. For the true story is so entirely different from the false official story that the official classes tell that by this time the working class itself has largely forgotten its own experience. Either story can be quite logically linked up with Female Suffrage, which, therefore, I leave where it is for the moment; merely confessing that, so long as we get hold of the right story and not the wrong story, it seems to me a matter of secondary importance whether we link it up with Female Suffrage or not.

Now the ordinary version of recent English history that most moderately educated people have absorbed from childhood is something like this. That we emerged slowly from a semi-barbarism in which all the power and wealth were in the hands of Kings and a few nobles; that the King's power was broken first and then in due time that of the nobles, that this piece-meal improvement was brought about by one class after another waking up to a sense of citizenship and demanding a place in the national councils, frequently by riot or violence; and that in consequence of such menacing popular action, the franchise was granted to one class after another and used more and more to improve the social conditions of those classes, until we practically became a democracy, save for such exceptions as that of the women. I do not think anyone will deny that something like that is the general idea of the educated man who reads a newspaper and of the newspaper that he reads. That is the view current at public schools and colleges; it is part of the culture of all the classes that count for much in government; and there is not one word of truth in it from beginning to end.

That Great Reform Bill

Wealth and political power were very much more popularly distributed in the Middle Ages than they are now; but we will pass all that and consider recent history. The franchise has never been largely and liberally granted in England; half the males have no vote and are not likely to get one. It was *never* granted in reply to pressure from awakened sections of the democracy; in every case there was a perfectly clear motive for granting it solely for the convenience of the aristocrats. The Great Reform Bill was not passed in response to such riots as that which destroyed a Castle; nor did the men who destroyed the Castle get any advantage whatever out of the Great Reform Bill. The Great Reform Bill was passed in order to seal an alliance between the landed aristocrats and the rich manufacturers of the north (an alliance that rules us still); and the chief object of that alliance was to *prevent* the English populace getting any political power in the general excitement after the French Revolution. No one can read Macaulay's speech on the Chartists, for instance, and not see that this is so. Disraeli's further extension of the suffrage was not effected by the intellectual vivacity and pure republican theory of the mid-Victorian agricultural labourer; it was effected by a politician who saw an opportunity to dish the Whigs, and guessed that certain orthodoxies in the more prosperous artisan might yet give him a balance against the commercial Radicals. And while this very thin game of wire-pulling with the mere abstraction of the vote was being worked entirely by the oligarchs and entirely in their interests, the solid and real thing that was going on was the steady despoiling of the poor of all power or wealth, until they find themselves to-day upon the threshold of slavery. That is The Working Man's

History of England.

Now, as I have said, I care comparatively little what is done with the mere voting part of the matter, so long as it is not claimed in such a way as to allow the plutocrat to escape his responsibility for his crimes, by pretending to be much more progressive, or much more susceptible to popular protest, than he ever has been. And there is this danger in many of those who have answered me. One of them, for instance, says that women have been forced into their present industrial situations by the same iron economic laws that have compelled men. I say that men have not been compelled by iron economic laws, but in the main by the coarse and Christless cynicism of other men. But, of course, this way of talking is exactly in accordance with the fashionable and official version of English history. Thus, you will read that the monasteries, places where men of the poorest origin could be powerful, grew corrupt and gradually decayed. Or you will read that the mediaeval guilds of free workmen yielded at last to an inevitable economic law. You will read this; and you will be reading lies. They might as well say that Julius Caesar gradually decayed at the foot of Pompey's statue. You might as well say that Abraham Lincoln yielded at last to an inevitable economic law. The free mediaeval guilds did not decay; they were murdered. Solid men with solid guns and halberds, armed with lawful warrants from living statesmen broke up their corporations and took away their hard cash from them. In the same way the people in Cradley Heath are no more victims of a necessary economic law than the people in Putumayo. They are victims of a very terrible creature, of whose sins much has been said since the beginning of the world; and of whom it was said of old, "Let us fall into the hands of God, for His mercies are great; but let us not fall into the hands of Man."

The Capitalist is in the Dock

Now it is this offering of a false economic excuse for the sweater that is the danger in perpetually saying that the poor woman will use the vote and that the poor man has not used it. The poor man is prevented from using it; prevented by the rich man, and the poor woman would be prevented in exactly the same gross and stringent style. I do not deny, of course, that there is something in the English temperament, and in the heritage of the last few centuries that makes the English workman more tolerant of wrong than most foreign workmen would be. But this only slightly modifies the main fact of the moral responsibility. To take an imperfect parallel, if we said that negro slaves would have rebelled if negroes had been more intelligent, we should be saying what is reasonable. But if we were to say that it could by any possibility be represented as being the negro's fault that he was at that moment in America and not in Africa, we should be saying what is frankly unreasonable. It is every bit as unreasonable to say the mere supineness of the English workmen has put them in the capitalist slave-yard. The capitalist has put them in the capitalist slaveyard; and very cunning smiths have hammered the chains. It is just this creative criminality in the authors of the system that we must not allow to be slurred over. The capitalist is in the dock to-day; and so far as I at least can prevent him, he shall not get out of it.

THE FRENCH REVOLUTION AND THE IRISH

It will be long before the poison of the Party System is worked out of the body politic. Some of its most indirect effects are the most dangerous. One that is very dangerous just now is this: that for most Englishmen the Party System falsifies history, and especially the history of revolutions. It falsifies history because it simplifies history. It paints everything either Blue or Buff in the style of its own silly circus politics: while a real revolution has as many colours as the sunrise—or the end of the world. And if we do not get rid of this error we shall make very bad blunders about the real revolution which seems to grow more and more probable, especially among the Irish. And any human familiarity with history will teach a man this first of all: that Party practically does not exist in a real revolution. It is a game for quiet times.

If you take a boy who has been to one of those big private schools which are falsely called the Public Schools, and another boy who has been to one of those large public schools which are falsely called the Board Schools, you will find some differences between the two, chiefly a difference in the management of the voice. But you will find they are both English in a special way, and that their education has been essentially the same. They are ignorant on the same subjects. They have never heard of the same plain facts. They have been taught the wrong answer to the same confusing question. There is one fundamental element in the attitude of the Eton master talking about "playing the game," and the elementary teacher training gutter-snipes to sing, "What is the Meaning of Empire Day?" And the name of that element is "unhistoric." It knows nothing really about England, still less about Ireland or France, and, least of all, of course, about anything like the French Revolution.

Revolution by Snap Division

Now what general notion does the ordinary English boy, thus taught to utter one ignorance in one of two accents, get and keep through life about the French Revolution? It is the notion of the English House of Commons with an enormous Radical majority on one side of the table and a small Tory minority on the other; the majority voting solid for a Republic, the minority voting solid for a Monarchy; two teams tramping through two lobbies with no difference between their methods and ours, except that (owing to some habit peculiar to Gaul) the brief intervals were brightened by a riot or a massacre, instead of by a whisky and soda and a Marconi tip. Novels are much more reliable than histories in such matters. For though an English novel about France does not tell the truth about France, it does tell the truth about England; and more than half the histories never tell the truth about anything. And popular fiction, I think, bears witness to the general English impression. The French Revolution is a snap division with an unusual turnover of votes. On the one side stand a king and queen who are good but weak, surrounded by nobles with rapiers drawn; some of whom are good, many of whom are wicked, all of whom are good-looking. Against these there is a formless mob of human beings, wearing red caps and seemingly insane, who all blindly follow ruffians who are also rhetoricians; some of whom die repentant and others unrepentant towards the end of the fourth act. The leaders of this boiling mass of all men melted into one are called Mirabeau, Robespierre, Danton, Marat, and so on. And it is conceded that their united frenzy may have been forced on them by the evils of the old regime.

That, I think, is the commonest English view of the French Revolution; and it will not survive the reading of two pages of any real speech or letter of the period. These human beings were human; varied, complex and inconsistent. But the rich Englishman, ignorant of revolutions, would hardly believe you if you told him some of the common human subtleties of the case. Tell him that Robespierre threw the red cap in the dirt in disgust, while the king had worn it with a broad grin, so to speak; tell him that Danton, the fierce founder of the Republic of the Terror, said quite sincerely to a noble, "I am more monarchist than you;" tell him that the Terror really seems to have been brought to an end chiefly by the efforts of people who particularly wanted to go on with it—and he will not believe these things. He will not believe them because he has no humility, and therefore no realism. He has never been inside himself; and so could never be inside another man. The truth is that in the French affair everybody occupied an individual position. Every man talked sincerely, if not because he was sincere, then because he was angry. Robespierre talked even more about God than about the Republic because he cared even more about God than about the Republic. Danton talked even more about France than about the Republic because he cared even more about France than about the Republic. Marat talked more about Humanity than either, because that physician (though himself somewhat needing a physician) really cared about it. The nobles were divided, each man from the next. The attitude of the king was quite different from the attitude of the queen; certainly much more different than any differences between our Liberals and Tories for the last twenty years. And it will sadden *some* of my friends to remember that it was the king who was the Liberal and the queen who was the Tory. There were not two people, I think, in that most practical crisis who stood in precisely the same attitude towards the situation. And that is why, between them, they saved Europe. It is when you really perceive the unity of mankind that you really perceive its variety. It is not a flippancy, it is a very sacred truth, to say that when men really understand that they are brothers they instantly begin to fight.

The Revival of Reality

Now these things are repeating themselves with an enormous reality in the Irish Revolution. You will not be able to make a Party System out of the matter. Everybody is in revolt; therefore everybody is telling the truth. The Nationalists will go on caring most for the nation, as Danton and the defenders of the frontier went on caring most for the nation. The priests will go on caring most for religion, as Robespierre went on caring most for religion. The Socialists will go on caring most for the cure of physical suffering, as Marat went on caring most for it. It is out of these real differences that real things can be made, such as the modern French democracy. For by such tenacity everyone sees at last that there is something in the other person's position. And those drilled in party discipline see nothing either past or present. And where there is nothing there is Satan.

For a long time past in our politics there has not only been no real battle, but no real bargain. No two men have bargained as Gladstone and Parnell bargained—each knowing the other to be a power. But in real revolutions men discover that no one man can really agree with another man until he has disagreed with him.

LIBERALISM: A SAMPLE

There is a certain daily paper in England towards which I feel very much as Tom Pinch felt towards Mr. Pecksniff immediately after he had found him out. The war upon Dickens was part of the general war on all democrats, about the eighties and nineties, which ushered in the brazen plutocracy of to-day. And one of the things that it was fashionable to say of Dickens in drawing-rooms was that he had no subtlety, and could not describe a complex frame of mind. Like most other things that are said in drawing-rooms, it was a lie. Dickens was a very unequal writer, and his successes alternate with his failures; but his successes are subtle quite as often as they are simple. Thus, to take "Martin Chuzzlewit" alone, I should call the joke about the Lord No-zoo a simple joke: but I should call the joke about Mrs. Todgers's vision of a wooden leg a subtle joke. And no frame of mind was ever so self-contradictory and yet so realistic as that which Dickens describes when he says, in effect, that, though Pinch knew now that there had never been such a person as Pecksniff, in his ideal sense, he could not bring himself to insult the very face and form that had contained the legend. The parallel with Liberal journalism is not perfect; because it was once honest; and Pecksniff presumably never was. And even when I come to feel a final incompatibility of temper, Pecksniff was not so Pecksniffian as he has since become. But the comparison is complete in so far as I share all the reluctance of Mr. Pinch. Some old heathen king was advised by one of the Celtic saints, I think, to burn what he had adored and adore what he had burnt. I am quite ready, if anyone will prove I was wrong, to adore what I have burnt; but I do really feel an unwillingness verging upon weakness to burning what I have adored. I think it is a weakness to be overcome in times as bad as these, when (as Mr. Orage wrote with something like splendid common sense the other day) there is such a lot to do and so few people who will do it. So I will devote this article to considering one case of the astounding baseness to which Liberal journalism has sunk.

Mental Breakdown in Fleet Street

One of the two or three streaks of light on our horizon can be perceived in this: that the moral breakdown of these papers has been accompanied by a mental breakdown also. The contemporary official paper, like the "Daily News" or the "Daily Chronicle" (I mean in so far as it deals with politics), simply cannot argue; and simply does not pretend to argue. It considers the solution which it imagines that wealthy people want, and it signifies the same in the usual manner; which is not by holding up its hand, but by falling on its face. But there is no more curious quality in its degradation than a sort of carelessness, at once of hurry and fatigue, with which it flings down its argument—or rather its refusal to argue. It does not even write sophistry: it writes anything. It does not so much poison the reader's mind as simply assume that the reader hasn't got one. For instance, one of these papers printed an article on Sir Stuart Samuel, who, having broken the great Liberal statute against corruption, will actually, perhaps, be asked to pay his own fine—in spite of the fact that he can well afford to do so. The article says, if I remember aright, that the decision will cause general surprise and some indignation. That any modern Government making a very rich capitalist obey the law will cause general surprise, may be true. Whether it will cause general indignation rather depends on whether our social intercourse is entirely confined to Park Lane, or any such pigsties built of gold. But the journalist proceeds to say, his neck rising higher and higher out of his collar, and his hair rising higher and higher on his head, in short, his resemblance to the Dickens' original increasing every instant, that he does not mean that the law against corruption should be less stringent, but that the burden should be borne by the whole community. This may mean that whenever a rich man breaks the law, all the poor men ought to be made to pay his fine. But I will suppose a slightly less insane meaning. I will suppose it means that the whole power of the commonwealth should be used to prosecute an offender of this kind. That, of course, can only mean that the matter will be decided by that instrument which still pretends to represent the whole power of the commonwealth. In other words, the Government will judge the Government.

Now this is a perfectly plain piece of brute logic. We need not go into the other delicious things in the article, as when it says that "in old times Parliament had to be protected against Royal invasion by the man in the street." Parliament has to be protected now against the man in the street. Parliament is simply the most detested and the most detestable of all our national institutions: all that is evident enough. What is interesting is the blank and staring fallacy of the attempted reply.

When the Journalist is Ruined

A long while ago, before all the Liberals died, a Liberal introduced a Bill to prevent Parliament being merely packed with the slaves of financial interests. For that purpose he established the excellent democratic principle that the private citizen, as such, might protest against public corruption. He was called the Common Informer. I believe the miserable party papers are really reduced to playing on the degradation of the two words in modern language. Now the word "common" in "Common Informer" means exactly what it means in "common sense" or "Book of Common Prayer," or (above all) in "House of Commons." It does not mean anything low or vulgar; any more than they do. The only difference is that the House of Commons really is low and vulgar; and the Common Informer isn't. It is just the same with the word "Informer." It does not mean spy or sneak. It means one who gives information. It means what "journalist" ought to mean. The only difference is that the Common Informer may be paid if he tells the truth. The common journalist will be ruined if he does.

Now the quite plain point before the party journalist is this: If he really means that a corrupt bargain between a Government and a contractor ought to be judged by public opinion, he must (nowadays) mean Parliament; that is, the caucus that controls Parliament. And he must decide between one of two views. Either he means that there can be no such thing as a corrupt Government. Or he means that it is one of the characteristic qualities of a corrupt Government to denounce its own corruption. I laugh; and I leave him his choice.

THE FATIGUE OF FLEET STREET

Why is the modern party political journalism so bad? It is worse even than it intends to be. It praises its preposterous party leaders through thick and thin; but it somehow succeeds in making them look greater fools than they are. This clumsiness clings even to the photographs of public men, as they are snapshotted at public meetings. A sensitive politician (if there is such a thing) would, I should think, want to murder the man who snapshots him at those moments. For our general impression of a man's gesture or play of feature is made up of a series of vanishing instants, at any one of which he may look worse than our general impression records. Mr. Augustine Birrell may have made quite a sensible and amusing speech, in the course of which his audience would hardly have noticed that he resettled his necktie. Snapshot him, and he appears as convulsively clutching his throat in the agonies of strangulation, and with his head twisted on one side as if he had been hanged. Sir Edward Carson might make a perfectly good speech, which no one thought wearisome, but might himself be just tired enough to shift from one leg to the other. Snapshot him, and he appears as holding one leg stiffly in the air and yawning enough to swallow the audience. But it is in the prose narratives of the Press that we find most manifestations of this strange ineptitude; this knack of exhibiting your own favourites in an unlucky light. It is not so much that the party journalists do not tell the truth as that they tell just enough of it to make it clear that they are telling lies. One of their favourite blunders is an amazing sort of bathos. They begin by telling you that some statesman said something brilliant in style or biting in wit, at which his hearers thrilled with terror or thundered with applause. And then they tell you what it was that he said. Silly asses!

Insane Exaggeration

Here is an example from a leading Liberal paper touching the debates on Home Rule. I am a Home Ruler; so my sympathies would be, if anything, on the side of the Liberal paper upon that point. I merely quote it as an example of this ridiculous way of writing, which, by insane exaggeration, actually makes its hero look smaller than he is.

This was strange language to use about the "hypocritical sham," and Mr. Asquith, knowing that the biggest battle of his career was upon him, hit back without mercy. "I should like first to know," said he, with a glance at his supporters, "whether my proposals are accepted?"

That's all. And I really do not see why poor Mr. Asquith should be represented as having violated the Christian virtue of mercy by saying that. I myself could compose a great many paragraphs upon the same model, each containing its stinging and perhaps unscrupulous epigram. As, for example:—"The Archbishop of Canterbury, realising that his choice now lay between denying God and earning the crown of martyrdom by dying in torments, spoke with a frenzy of religious passion that might have seemed fanatical under circumstances less intense. 'The Children's Service,' he said firmly, with his face to the congregation, 'will be held at half-past four this afternoon as usual.'"

Or, we might have:—"Lord Roberts, recognising that he had now to face Armageddon, and that if he lost this last battle against overwhelming odds the independence of England would be extinguished forever, addressed to his soldiers (looking at them and not falling off his horse) a speech which brought their national passions to boiling point, and might well have seemed blood-thirsty in quieter times. It ended with the celebrated declaration that it was a fine day."

Or we might have the much greater excitement of reading something like this:—"The Astronomer Royal, having realised that the earth would certainly be smashed to pieces by a comet unless his requests in connection with wireless telegraphy were seriously considered, gave an address at the Royal Society which, under other circumstances, would have seemed unduly dogmatic and emotional and deficient in scientific agnosticism. This address (which he delivered without any attempt to stand on his head) included a fierce and even ferocious declaration that it is generally easier to see the stars by night than by day."

Now, I cannot see, on my conscience and reason, that any one of my imaginary paragraphs is more ridiculous than the real one. Nobody can believe that Mr. Asquith regards these belated and careful compromises about Home Rule as "the biggest battle of his career." It is only justice to him to say that he has had bigger battles than that. Nobody can believe that any body of men, bodily present, either thundered or thrilled at a man merely saying that he would like to know whether his proposals were accepted. No; it would be far better for Parliament if its doors were shut again, and reporters were excluded. In that case, the outer public did hear genuine rumours of almost gigantic eloquence; such as that which has perpetuated Pitt's reply against the charge of youth, or Fox's bludgeoning of the idea of war as a compromise. It would be much better to follow the old fashion and let in no reporters at all than to follow the new fashion and select the stupidest reporters you can find.

Their Load of Lies

Now, why do people in Fleet-street talk such tosh? People in Fleet-street are not fools. Most of them have realised reality through work; some through starvation; some through damnation, or something damnably like it. I think it is simply and seriously true that they are tired of their job. As the general said in M. Rostand's play, "la fatigue!"

I do really believe that this is one of the ways in which God (don't get flurried, Nature if you like) is unexpectedly avenged on things infamous and unreasonable. And this method is that men's moral and even physical tenacity actually give out under such a load of lies. They go on writing their leading articles and their Parliamentary reports. They go on doing it as a convict goes on picking oakum. But the point is not that we are bored with their articles; the point is that they are.

The work is done worse because it is done weakly and without human enthusiasm. And it is done weakly because of the truth we have told so many times in this book: that it is not done for monarchy, for which men will die; or for democracy, for which men will die; or even for aristocracy, for which many men have died. It is done for a thing called Capitalism: which stands out quite clearly in history in many curious ways. But the most curious thing about it is that no man has loved it; and no man died for it.

THE AMNESTY FOR AGGRESSION

If there is to rise out of all this red ruin something like a republic of justice, it is essential that our views should be real views; that is, glimpses of lives and landscapes outside ourselves. It is essential that they should not be mere opium visions that begin and end in smoke—and so often in cannon smoke. I make no apology, therefore, for returning to the purely practical and realistic point I urged last week: the fact that we shall lose everything we might have gained if we lose the idea that the responsible person is responsible.

For instance, it is almost specially so with the one or two things in which the British Government, or the British public, really are behaving badly. The first, and worst of them, is the non-extension of the Moratorium, or truce of debtor and creditor, to the very world where there are the poorest debtors and the cruellest creditors. This is infamous: and should be, if possible, more infamous to those who think the war right than to those who think it wrong. Everyone knows that the people who can least pay their debts are the people who are always trying to. Among the poor a payment may be as rash as a speculation. Among the rich a bankruptcy may be as safe as a bank. Considering the class from which private soldiers are taken, there is an atrocious meanness in the idea of buying their blood abroad, while we sell their sticks at home. The English language, by the way, is full of delicate paradoxes. We talk of the private soldiers because they are really public soldiers; and we talk of the public schools because they are really private schools. Anyhow, the wrong is of the sort that ought to be resisted, as much in war as in peace.

Ought to Be Hammered

But as long as we speak of it as a cloudy conclusion, come to by an anonymous club called Parliament, or a masked tribunal called the Cabinet, we shall never get such a wrong righted. Somebody is officially responsible for the unfairness; and that somebody ought to be hammered. The other example, less important but more ludicrous, is the silly boycott of Germans in England, extending even to German music. I do not believe for a moment that the English people feel any such insane fastidiousness. Are the English artists who practise the particularly English art of water-colour to be forbidden to use Prussian blue? Are all old ladies to shoot their Pomeranian dogs? But though England would laugh at this, she will get the credit of it, and will continue: until we ask who the actual persons are who feel sure that we should shudder at a ballad of the Rhine. It is certain that we should find they are capitalists. It is very probable that we should find they are foreigners.

Some days ago the Official Council of the Independent Labour Party, or the Independent Council of the Official Labour Party, or the Independent and Official Council of the Labour Party (I have got quite nervous about these names and distinctions; but they all seem to say the same thing) began their manifesto by saying it would be difficult to assign the degrees of responsibility which each nation had for the outbreak of the war. Afterwards, a writer in the "Christian Commonwealth," lamenting war in the name of Labour, but in the language of my own romantic middle-class, said that all the nations must share the responsibility for this great calamity of war. Now exactly as long as we go on talking like that we shall have war after war, and calamity after calamity, until the crack of doom. It simply amounts to a promise of pardon to any person who will start a quarrel. It is an amnesty for assassins. The moment any man assaults any other man he makes all the other men as bad as himself. He has only to stab, and to vanish in a fog of forgetfulness. The real eagles of iron, the predatory Empires, will be delighted with this doctrine. They will applaud the

Labour Concert or Committee, or whatever it is called. They will willingly take all the crime, with only a quarter of the conscience: they will be as ready to share the memory as they are to share the spoil. The Powers will divide responsibility as calmly as they divided Poland.

The Whole Loathsome Load

But I still stubbornly and meekly submit my point: that you cannot end war without asking who began it. If you think somebody else, not Germany, began it, then blame that somebody else: do not blame everybody and nobody. Perhaps you think that a small sovereign people, fresh from two triumphant wars, ought to discrown itself before sunrise; because the nephew of a neighbouring Emperor has been shot by his own subjects. Very well. Then blame Servia; and, to the extent of your influence, you may be preventing small kingdoms being obstinate or even princes being shot. Perhaps you think the whole thing was a huge conspiracy of Russia, with France as a dupe and Servia as a pretext. Very well. Then blame Russia; and, to the extent of your influence, you may be preventing great Empires from making racial excuses for a raid. Perhaps you think France wrong for feeling what you call "revenge," and I should call recovery of stolen goods. Perhaps you blame Belgium for being sentimental about her frontier; or England for being sentimental about her word. If so, blame them; or whichever of them you think is to blame. Or again, it is barely possible that you may think, as I do, that the whole loathsome load has been laid upon us by the monarchy which I have not named; still less wasted time in abusing. But if there be in Europe a military State which has not the religion of Russia, yet has helped Russia to tyrannise over the Poles, that State cares not for religion, but for tyranny. If there be a State in Europe which has not the religion of the Austrians, but has helped Austria to bully the Servians, that State cares not for belief, but for bullying. If there be in Europe any people or principality which respects neither republics nor religions, to which the political ideal of Paris is as much a myth as the mystical ideal of Moscow, then blame that: and do more than blame. In the healthy and highly theological words of Robert Blatchford, drive it back to the Hell from which it came.

Crying Over Spilt Blood

But whatever you do, do not blame everybody for what was certainly done by somebody. It may be it is no good crying over spilt blood, any more than over spilt milk. But we do not find the culprit any more by spilling the milk over everybody; or by daubing everybody with blood. Still less do we improve matters by watering the milk with our tears, nor the blood either. To say that everybody is responsible means that nobody is responsible. If in the future we see Russia annexing Rutland (as part of the old Kingdom of Muscovy), if we see Bavaria taking a sudden fancy to the Bank of England, or the King of the Cannibal Islands suddenly demanding a tribute of edible boys and girls from England and America, we may be quite certain also that the Leader of the Labour Party will rise, with a slight cough, and say: "It would be a difficult task to apportion the blame between the various claims which..."

REVIVE THE COURT JESTER

I hope the Government will not think just now about appointing a Poet Laureate. I hardly think they can be altogether in the right mood. The business just now before the country makes a very good detective story; but as a national epic it is a little depressing. Jingo literature always weakens a nation; but even healthy patriotic literature has its proper time and occasion. For instance, Mr. Newbolt (who has been suggested for the post) is a very fine poet; but I think his patriotic lyrics would just now rather jar upon a patriot. We are rather too much concerned about our practical seamanship to feel quite confident that Drake will return and "drum them up the Channel as he drummed them long ago." On the contrary, we have an uncomfortable feeling that Drake's ship might suddenly go to the bottom, because the capitalists have made Lloyd George abolish the Plimsoll Line. One could not, without being understood ironically, adjure the two party teams to-day to "play up, play up and play the game," or to "love the game more than the prize." And there is no national hero at this moment in the soldiering line—unless, perhaps, it is Major Archer-Shee—of whom anyone would be likely to say: "Sed miles; sed pro patria." There is, indeed, one beautiful poem of Mr. Newbolt's which may mingle faintly with one's thoughts in such times, but that, alas, is to a very different tune. I mean that one in which he echoes Turner's conception of the old wooden ship vanishing with all the valiant memories of the English:

There's a far bell ringing At the setting of the sun, And a phantom voice is singing Of the great days done. There's a far bell ringing, And a phantom voice is singing Of a fame forever clinging To the great days done. For the sunset breezes shiver, Temeraire, Temeraire, And she's fading down the river....

Well, well, neither you nor I know whether she is fading down the river or not. It is quite enough for us to know, as King Alfred did, that a great many pirates have landed on both banks of the Thames.

Praise and Prophecy Impossible

At this moment that is the only kind of patriotic poem that could satisfy the emotions of a patriotic person. But it certainly is not the sort of poem that is expected from a Poet Laureate, either on the highest or the lowest theory of his office. He is either a great minstrel singing the victories of a great king, or he is a common Court official like the Groom of the Powder Closet. In the first case his praises should be true; in the second case they will nearly always be false; but in either case he must praise. And what there is for him to praise just now it would be precious hard to say. And if there is no great hope of a real poet, there is still less hope of a real prophet. What Newman called, I think, "The Prophetical Office," that is, the institution of an inspired protest even against an inspired religion, certainly would not do in modern England. The Court is not likely to keep a tame prophet in order to encourage him to be wild. It is not likely to pay a man to say that wolves shall howl in Downing-street and vultures build their nests in Buckingham Palace. So vast has been the progress of humanity that these two things are quite impossible. We cannot have a great poet praising kings. We cannot have a great prophet denouncing kings. So I have to fall back on a third suggestion.

The Field for a Fool

Instead of reviving the Court Poet, why not revive the Court Fool? He is the only person who could do any good at this moment either to the Royal or the judicial Courts. The present political situation is utterly unsuitable for the purposes of a great poet. But it is particularly suitable for the purposes of a great buffoon. The old jester was under certain privileges: you could not resent the jokes of a fool, just as you cannot resent the sermons of a curate. Now, what the present Government of England wants is neither serious praise nor serious denunciation; what it wants is satire. What it wants, in other words, is realism given with gusto. When King Louis the Eleventh unexpectedly visited his enemy, the Duke of Burgundy, with a small escort, the Duke's jester said he would give the King his fool's cap, for he was the fool now. And when the Duke replied with dignity, "And suppose I treat him with all proper respect?" the fool answered, "Then I will give it to you." That is the kind of thing that somebody ought to be free to say now. But if you say it now you will be fined a hundred pounds at the least.

Carson's Dilemma

For the things that have been happening lately are not merely things that one could joke about. They are themselves, truly and intrinsically, jokes. I mean that there is a sort of epigram of unreason in the situation itself, as there was in the situation where there was jam yesterday and jam to-morrow but never jam to-day. Take, for instance, the extraordinary case of Sir Edward Carson. The point is not whether we regard his attitude in Belfast as the defiance of a sincere and dogmatic rebel, or as the bluff of a party hack and mountebank. The point is not whether we regard his defence of the Government at the Old Bailey as a chivalrous and reluctant duty done as an advocate or a friend, or as a mere case of a lawyer selling his soul for a fat brief. The point is that whichever of the two actions we approve, and whichever of the four explanations we adopt, Sir Edward's position is still raving nonsense. On any argument, he cannot escape from his dilemma. It may be argued that laws and customs should be obeyed whatever our private feelings; and that it is an established custom to accept a brief in such a case. But then it is a somewhat more established custom to obey an Act of Parliament and to keep the peace. It may be argued that extreme misgovernment justifies men in Ulster or elsewhere in refusing to obey the law. But then it would justify them even more in refusing to appear professionally in a law court. Etiquette cannot be at once so unimportant that Carson may shoot at the King's uniform, and yet so important that he must always be ready to put on his own. The Government cannot be so disreputable that Carson need not lay down his gun, and yet so respectable that he is bound to put on his wig. Carson cannot at once be so fierce that he can kill in what he considers a good cause, and yet so meek that he must argue in what he considers a bad cause. Obedience or disobedience, conventional or unconventional, a solicitor's letter cannot be more sacred than the King's writ; a blue bag cannot be more rational than the British flag. The thing is rubbish read anyway, and the only difficulty is to get a joke good enough to express it. It is a case for the Court Jester. The phantasy of it could only be expressed by some huge ceremonial hoax. Carson ought to be crowned with the shamrocks and emeralds and followed by green-clad minstrels of the Clan-na-Gael, playing "The Wearing of the Green."

Belated Chattiness by Wireless

But all the recent events are like that. They are practical jokes. The jokes do not need to be made: they only need to be pointed out. You and I do not talk and act as the Isaacs brothers talked and acted, by their own most favourable account of themselves; and even their account of themselves was by no means favourable. You and I do not talk of meeting our own born brother "at a family function" as if he were some infinitely distant cousin whom we only met at Christmas. You and I, when we suddenly feel inclined for a chat with the same brother about his dinner and the Coal Strike, do not generally select either wireless telegraphy or the Atlantic Cable as the most obvious and economical channel for that outburst of belated chattiness. You and I do not talk, if it is proposed to start a railway between Catsville and Dogtown, as if the putting up of a station at Dogtown could have no kind of economic effect on the putting up of a station at Catsville. You and I do not think it candid to say that when we are at one end of a telephone we have no sort of connection with the other end. These things have got into the region of farce; and should be dealt with farcically, not even ferociously.

A Fool Who Shall Be Free

In the Roman Republic there was a Tribune of the People, whose person was inviolable like an ambassador's. There was much the same idea in Becket's attempt to remove the Priest, who was then the popular champion, from the ordinary courts. We shall have no Tribune; for we have no republic. We shall have no Priest; for we have no religion. The best we deserve or can expect is a Fool who shall be free; and who shall deliver us with laughter.

THE ART OF MISSING THE POINT

Missing the point is a very fine art; and has been carried to something like perfection by politicians and Pressmen to-day. For the point is generally a very sharp point; and is, moreover, sharp at both ends. That is to say that both parties would probably impale themselves in an uncomfortable manner if they did not manage to avoid it altogether. I have just been looking at the election address of the official Liberal candidate for the part of the country in which I live; and though it is, if anything, rather more logical and free from cant than most other documents of the sort it is an excellent example of missing the point. The candidate has to go boring on about Free Trade and Land Reform and Education; and nobody reading it could possibly imagine that in the town of Wycombe, where the poll will be declared, the capital of the Wycombe division of Bucks which the candidate is contesting, centre of the important and vital trade on which it has thriven, a savage struggle about justice has been raging for months past between the poor and rich, as real as the French Revolution. The man offering himself at Wycombe as representative of the Wycombe division simply says nothing about it at all. It is as if a man at the crisis of the French Terror had offered himself as a deputy for the town of Paris, and had said nothing about the Monarchy, nothing about the Republic, nothing about the massacres, nothing about the war; but had explained with great clearness his views on the suppression of the Jansenists, the literary style of Racine, the suitability of Turenae for the post of commander-in-chief, and the religious reflections of Madame de Maintenon. For, at their best, the candidate's topics are not topical. Home Rule is a very good thing, and modern education is a very bad thing; but neither of them are things that anybody is talking about in High Wycombe. This is the first and simplest way of missing the point: deliberately to avoid and ignore it.

The Candid Candidate

It would be an amusing experiment, by the way, to go to the point instead of avoiding it. What fun it would be to stand as a strict Party candidate, but issue a perfectly frank and cynical Election Address. Mr. Mosley's address begins, "Gentlemen,—Sir Alfred Cripps having been chosen for a high judicial position and a seat in the House of Lords, a by-election now becomes necessary, and the electors of South Bucks are charged with the responsible duty of electing, etc., etc." But suppose there were another candidate whose election address opened in a plain, manly style, like this: "Gentlemen,—In the sincere hope of being myself chosen for a high judicial position or a seat in the House of Lords, or considerably increasing my private fortune by some Government appointment, or, at least, inside information about the financial prospects, I have decided that it is worth my while to disburse large sums of money to you on various pretexts, and, with even more reluctance to endure the bad speaking and bad ventilation of the Commons' House of Parliament, so help me God. I have very pronounced convictions on various political questions; but I will not trouble my fellow-citizens with them, since I have quite made up my mind to abandon any or all of them if requested to do so by the upper classes. The electors are therefore charged with the entirely irresponsible duty of electing a Member; or, in other words, I ask my neighbours round about this part, who know I am not a bad chap in many ways, to do me a good turn in my business, just as I might ask them to change a sovereign. My election will have no conceivable kind of effect on anything or anybody except myself; so I ask, as man to man, the Electors of the Southern or Wycombe Division of the County of Buckingham to accept a ride in one of my motor-cars; and poll early to please a pal—God Save the King." I do not know whether you or I would be elected if we presented ourselves with an election address of that kind; but we should have had our fun and (comparatively speaking) saved our souls; and I have a strong suspicion that we should be elected or rejected on a mechanical majority like anybody else; nobody having dreamed of reading an election address any more than an advertisement of a hair restorer.

Tyranny and Head-Dress

But there is another and more subtle way in which we may miss the point; and that is, not by keeping a dead silence about it, but by being just witty enough to state it wrong. Thus, some of the Liberal official papers have almost screwed up their courage to the sticking-point about the bestial coup d'etat in South Africa. They have screwed up their courage to the sticking-point; and it has stuck. It cannot get any further; because it has missed the main point. The modern Liberals make their feeble attempts to attack the introduction of slavery into South Africa by the Dutch and the Jews, by a very typical evasion of the vital fact. The vital fact is simply slavery. Most of these Dutchmen have always felt like slave-owners. Most of these Jews have always felt like slaves. Now that they are on top, they have a particular and curious kind of impudence, which is only known among slaves. But the Liberal journalists will do their best to suggest that the South African wrong consisted in what they call Martial Law. That is, that there is something specially wicked about men doing an act of cruelty in khaki or in vermilion, but not if it is done in dark blue with pewter buttons. The tyrant who wears a busby or a forage cap is abominable; the tyrant who wears a horsehair wig is excusable. To be judged by soldiers is hell; but to be judged by lawyers is paradise.

Now the point must not be missed in this way. What is wrong with the tyranny in Africa is not that it is run by soldiers. It would be quite as bad, or worse, if it were run by policemen. What is wrong is that, for the first time since Pagan times, private men are being forced to work for a private man. Men are being punished by imprisonment or exile for refusing to accept a job. The fact that Botha can ride on a horse, or fire off a gun, makes him better rather than worse than any man like Sidney Webb or Philip Snowden, who attempt the same slavery by much less manly methods. The Liberal Party will try to divert the whole discussion to one about what they call militarism. But the very terms of modern politics contradict it. For when we talk of real rebels against the present system we call them Militants. And there will be none in the Servile State.

THE SERVILE STATE AGAIN

I read the other day, in a quotation from a German newspaper, the highly characteristic remark that Germany having annexed Belgium would soon re-establish its commerce and prosperity, and that, in particular, arrangements were already being made for introducing into the new province the German laws for the protection of workmen.

I am quite content with that paragraph for the purpose of any controversy about what is called German atrocity. If men I know had not told me they had themselves seen the bayoneting of a baby; if the most respectable refugees did not bring with them stories of burning cottages—yes, and of burning cottagers as well; if doctors did not report what they do report of the condition of girls in the hospitals; if there were no facts; if there were no photographs, that one phrase I have quoted would be quite sufficient to satisfy me that the Prussians are tyrants; tyrants in a peculiar and almost insane sense which makes them pre-eminent among the evil princes of the earth. The first and most striking feature is a stupidity that rises into a sort of ghastly innocence. The protection of workmen! Some workmen, perhaps, might have a fancy for being protected from shrapnel; some might be glad to put up an umbrella that would ward off things dropping from the gentle Zeppelin in heaven upon the place beneath. Some of these discontented proletarians have taken the same view as Vandervelde their leader, and are now energetically engaged in protecting themselves along the line of the Yser; I am glad to say not altogether without success. It is probable that nearly all of the Belgian workers would, on the whole, prefer to be protected against bombs, sabres, burning cities, starvation, torture, and the treason of wicked kings. In short, it is probable—it is at least possible, impious as is the idea—that they would prefer to be protected against Germans and all they represent. But if a Belgian workman is told that he is not to be protected against Germans, but actually to be protected by Germans, I think he may be excused for staring. His first impulse, I imagine, will be to ask, "Against whom? Are there any worse people to come along?"

But apart from the hellish irony of this humanitarian idea, the question it raises is really one of solid importance for people whose politics are more or less like ours. There is a very urgent point in that question, "Against whom would the Belgian workmen be protected by the German laws?" And if we pursue it, we shall be enabled to analyse something of that poison—very largely a Prussian poison—which has long been working in our own commonwealth, to the enslavement of the weak and the secret strengthening of the strong. For the Prussian armies are, pre-eminently, the advance guard of the Servile State. I say this scientifically, and quite apart from passion or even from preference. I have no illusions about either Belgium or England. Both have been stained with the soot of Capitalism and blinded with the smoke of mere Colonial ambition; both have been caught at a disadvantage in such modern dirt and disorder; both have come out much better than I should have expected countries so modern and so industrial to do. But in England and Belgium there is Capitalism mixed up with a great many other things, strong things and things that pursue other aims; Clericalism, for instance, and militant Socialism in Belgium; Trades Unionism and sport and the remains of real aristocracy in England. But Prussia is Capitalism; that is, a gradually solidifying slavery; and that majestic unity with which she moves, dragging all the dumb Germanies after her, is due to the fact that her Servile State is complete, while ours is incomplete. There are not mutinies; there are not even mockeries; the voice of national self-criticism has been extinguished forever. For this people is already permanently cloven into a higher and a lower class: in its industry as much as its army. Its employers are, in the strictest and most sinister sense, captains of industry. Its proletariat is, in the truest and most pitiable sense, an army of labour. In that atmosphere masters bear upon them the signs that they are more than men; and to insult an officer is death.

If anyone ask how this extreme and unmistakable subordination of the employed to the employers is brought about, we all know the answer. It is brought about by hunger and hardness of heart, accelerated by a certain kind of legislation, of which we have had a good deal lately in England, but which was almost invariably borrowed from Prussia. Mr. Herbert Samuel's suggestion that the poor should be able to put their money in little boxes and not be able to get it out again is a sort of standing symbol of all the rest. I have forgotten how the poor were going to benefit eventually by what is for them indistinguishable from dropping sixpence down a drain. Perhaps they were going to get it back some day; perhaps when they could produce a hundred coupons out of the Daily Citizen; perhaps when they got their hair cut; perhaps when they consented to be inoculated, or trepanned, or circumcised, or something. Germany is full of this sort of legislation; and if you asked an innocent German, who honestly believed in it, what it was, he would answer that it was for the protection of workmen.

And if you asked again "Their protection from what?" you would have the whole plan and problem of the Servile State plain in front of you. Whatever notion there is, there is no notion whatever of protecting the employed person *from his employer*. Much less is there any idea of his ever being anywhere except under an employer. Whatever the Capitalist wants he gets. He may have the sense to want washed and well-fed labourers rather than dirty and feeble ones, and the restrictions may happen to exist in the form of laws from the Kaiser or by-laws from the Krupps. But the Kaiser will not offend the Krupps, and the Krupps will not offend the Kaiser. Laws of this kind, then, do not attempt to protect workmen against the injustice of the Capitalist as the English Trade Unions did. They do not attempt to protect workmen against the injustice of the State as the mediaeval guilds did. Obviously they cannot protect workmen against the foreign invader—especially when (as in the comic case of Belgium) they are imposed by the foreign invader. What then are such laws designed to protect workmen against? Tigers, rattlesnakes, hyenas?

Oh, my young friends; oh, my Christian brethren, they are designed to protect this poor person from something which to those of established rank is more horrid than many hyenas. They are designed, my friends, to protect a man from himself—from something that the masters of the earth fear more than famine or war, and which Prussia especially fears as everything fears that which would certainly be its end. They are meant to protect a man against himself—that is, they are meant to protect a man against his manhood.

And if anyone reminds me that there is a Socialist Party in Germany, I reply that there isn't.

THE EMPIRE OF THE IGNORANT

That anarchic future which the more timid Tories professed to fear has already fallen upon us. We are ruled by ignorant people. But the most ignorant people in modern Britain are to be found in the upper class, the middle class, and especially the upper middle class. I do not say it with the smallest petulance or even distaste; these classes are often really beneficent in their breeding or their hospitality, or their humanity to animals.

There is still no better company than the young at the two Universities, or the best of the old in the Army or some of the other services. Also, of course, there are exceptions in the matter of learning; real scholars like Professor Gilbert Murray or Professor Phillimore are not ignorant, though they *are* gentlemen. But when one looks up at any mass of the wealthier and more powerful classes, at the Grand Stand at Epsom, at the windows of Park-lane, at the people at a full-dress debate or a fashionable wedding, we shall be safe in saying that they are, for the most part, the most ill-taught, or untaught, creatures in these islands.

Literally Illiterate

It is indeed their feeble boast that they are not literally illiterate. They are always saying the ancient barons could not sign their own names—for they know less of history perhaps than of anything else. The modern barons, however, can sign their own names—or someone else's for a change. They can sign their own names; and that is about all they can do. They cannot face a fact, or follow an argument, or feel a tradition; but, least of all, can they, upon any persuasion, read through a plain impartial book, English or foreign, that is not specially written to soothe their panic or to please their pride. Looking up at these seats of the mighty I can only say, with something of despair, what Robert Lowe said of the enfranchised workmen: "We must educate our masters."

I do not mean this as paradoxical, or even as symbolical; it is simply tame and true. The modern English rich know nothing about things, not even about the things to which they appeal. Compared with them, the poor are pretty sure to get some enlightenment, even if they cannot get liberty; they must at least be technical. An old apprentice learnt a trade, even if his master came like any Turk and banged him most severely. The old housewife knew which side her bread was buttered, even if it were so thin as to be almost imperceptible. The old sailor knew the ropes; even if he knew the rope's end. Consequently, when any of these revolted, they were concerned with things they knew, pains, practical impossibilities, or the personal record.

But They Know

The apprentice cried "Clubs?" and cracked his neighbours' heads with the precision and fineness of touch which only manual craftsmanship can give. The housewives who flatly refused to cook the hot dinner knew how much or how little, cold meat there was in the house. The sailor who defied discipline by mutinying at the Nore did not defy discipline in the sense of falling off the rigging or letting the water into the hold. Similarly the modern proletariat, however little it may know, knows what it is talking about.

But the curious thing about the educated class is that exactly what it does not know is what it is talking about. I mean that it is startlingly ignorant of those special things which it is supposed to invoke and keep inviolate. The things that workmen invoke may be uglier, more acrid, more sordid; but they know all about them. They know enough arithmetic to know that prices have risen; the kind Levantine gentleman is always there to make them fully understand the meaning of an interest sum; and the landlord will define Rent as rigidly as Ricardo. The doctors can always tell them the Latin for an empty stomach; and when the poor man is treated for the time with some human respect (by the Coronet) it almost seems a pity he is not alive to hear how legally he died.

Against this bitter shrewdness and bleak realism in the suffering classes it is commonly supposed that the more leisured classes stand for certain legitimate ideas which also have their place in life; such as history, reverence, the love of the land. Well, it might be no bad thing to have something, even if it were something narrow, that testified to the truths of religion or patriotism. But such narrow things in the past have always at least known their own history; the bigot knew his catechism; the patriot knew his way home. The astonishing thing about the modern rich is their real and sincere ignorance—especially of the things they like.

No!

Take the most topical case you can find in any drawing-room: Belfast. Ulster is most assuredly a matter of history; and there is a sense in which Orange resistance is a matter of religion. But go and ask any of the five hundred fluttering ladies at a garden party (who find Carson so splendid and Belfast so thrilling) what it is all about, when it began, where it came from, what it really maintains? What was the history of Ulster? What is the religion of Belfast? Do any of them know where Ulstermen were in Grattan's time; do any of them know what was the "Protestantism" that came from Scotland to that isle; could any of them tell what part of the old Catholic system it really denied?

It was generally something that the fluttering ladies find in their own Anglican churches every Sunday. It were vain to ask them to state the doctrines of the Calvinist creed; they could not state the doctrines of their own creed. It were vain to tell them to read the history of Ireland; they have never read the history of England. It would matter as little that they do not know these things, as that I do not know German; but then German is not the only thing I am supposed to know. History and ritual are the only things aristocrats are supposed to know; and they don't know them.

Smile and Smile

I am not fed on turtle soup and Tokay because of my exquisite intimacy with the style and idiom of Heine and Richter. The English governing class is fed on turtle soup and Tokay to represent the past, of which it is literally ignorant, as I am of German irregular verbs; and to represent the religious traditions of the State, when it does not know three words of theology, as I do not know three words of German.

This is the last insult offered by the proud to the humble. They rule them by the smiling terror of an ancient secret. They smile and smile; but they have forgotten the secret.

THE SYMBOLISM OF KRUPP

The curious position of the Krupp firm in the awful story developing around us is not quite sufficiently grasped. There is a kind of academic clarity of definition which does not see the proportions of things for which everything falls within a definition, and nothing ever breaks beyond it. To this type of mind (which is valuable when set to its special and narrow work) there is no such thing as an exception that proves the rule. If I vote for confiscating some usurer's millions I am doing, they say, precisely what I should be doing if I took pennies out of a blind man's hat. They are both denials of the principle of private property, and are equally right and equally wrong, according to our view of that principle. I should find a great many distinctions to draw in such a matter. First, I should say that taking a usurer's money by proper authority is not robbery, but recovery of stolen goods. Second, I should say that even if there were no such thing as personal property, there would still be such a thing as personal dignity, and different modes of robbery would diminish it in very different ways. Similarly, there is a truth, but only a half-truth, in the saying that all modern Powers alike rely on the Capitalist and make war on the lines of Capitalism. It is true, and it is disgraceful. But it is *not* equally true and equally disgraceful. It is not true that Montenegro is as much ruled by financiers as Prussia, just as it is not true that as many men in the Kaiserstrasse, in Berlin, wear long knives in their belts as wear them in the neighbourhood of the Black Mountain. It is not true that every peasant from one of the old Russian communes is the immediate servant of a rich man, as is every employee of Mr. Rockefeller. It is as false as the statement that no poor people in America can read or write. There is an element of Capitalism in all modern countries, as there is an element of illiteracy in all modern countries. There are some who think that the number of our fellow-citizens who can sign their names ought to comfort us for the extreme fewness of those who have anything in the bank to sign it for, but I am not one of these.

In any case, the position of Krupp has certain interesting aspects. When we talk of Army contractors as among the base but active actualities of war, we commonly mean that while the contractor benefits by the war, the war, on the whole, rather suffers by the contractor. We regard this unsoldierly middleman with disgust, or great anger, or contemptuous acquiescence, or commercial dread and silence, according to our personal position and character. But we nowhere think of him as having anything to do with fighting in the final sense. Those worthy and wealthy persons who employ women's labour at a few shillings a week do not do it to obtain the best clothes for the soldiers, but to make a sufficient profit on the worst. The only argument is whether such clothes are just good enough for the soldiers, or are too bad for anybody or anything. We tolerate the contractor, or we do not tolerate him; but no one admires him especially, and certainly no one gives him any credit for any success in the war. Confessedly or unconfessedly we knock his profits, not only off what goes to the taxpayer, but what goes to the soldier. We know the Army will not fight any better, at least, because the clothes they wear were stitched by wretched women who could hardly see; or because their boots were made by harassed helots, who never had time to think. In war-time it is very widely confessed that Capitalism is not a good way of ruling a patriotic or self-respecting people, and all sorts of other things, from strict State organisation to quite casual personal charity, are hastily substituted for it. It is recognised that the "great employer," nine times out of ten, is no more than the schoolboy or the page who pilfers tarts and sweets from the dishes as they go up and down. How angry one is with him depends on temperament, on the stage of the dinner—also on the number of tarts.

Now here comes in the real and sinister significance of Krupps. There are many capitalists in Europe as rich, as vulgar, as selfish, as rootedly opposed to any fellowship of the fortunate and unfortunate. But there is no other capitalist who claims, or can pretend to claim, that he has very appreciably *helped* the activities of his people in war. I will suppose that Lipton did not deserve the very severe criticisms made on his firm by Mr. Justice Darling; but, however blameless he was, nobody can suppose that British soldiers would charge better with the bayonet because they had some particular kind of groceries inside them. But Krupp can make a plausible claim that the huge infernal machines to which his country owes nearly all of its successes could only have been produced under the equally infernal conditions of the modern factory and the urban and proletarian civilisation. That is why the victory of Germany would be simply the victory of Krupp, and the victory of Krupp would be simply the victory of Capitalism. There, and there alone, Capitalism would be able to point to something done successfully for a whole nation—done (as it would certainly maintain) better than small free States or natural democracies could have done it. I confess I think the modern Germans morally second-rate, and I think that even war, when it is conducted most successfully by machinery, is second-rate war. But this second-rate war will become not only the first but the only brand, if the cannon of Krupp should conquer; and, what is very much worse, it will be the only intelligent answer that any capitalist has yet given against our case that Capitalism is as wasteful and as weak as it is certainly wicked. I do not fear any such finality, for I happen to believe in the kind of men who fight best with bayonets and whose fathers hammered their own pikes for the French Revolution.

THE TOWER OF BEBEL

Among the cloudy and symbolic stories in the beginning of the Bible there is one about a tower built with such vertical energy as to take a hold on heaven, but ruined and resulting only in a confusion of tongues. The story might be interpreted in many ways—religiously, as meaning that spiritual insolence starts all human separations; irreligiously, as meaning that the inhuman heavens grudge man his magnificent dream; or merely satirically as suggesting that all attempts to reach a higher agreement always end in more disagreement than there was before. It might be taken by the partially intelligent Kensitite as a judgment on Latin Christians for talking Latin. It might be taken by the somewhat less intelligent Professor Harnack as a final proof that all prehistoric humanity talked German. But when all was said, the symbol would remain that a plain tower, as straight as a sword, as simple as a lily, did nevertheless produce the deepest divisions that have been known among men. In any case we of the world in revolt—Syndicalists, Socialists, Guild Socialists, or whatever we call ourselves—have no need to worry about the scripture or the allegory. We have the reality. For whatever reason, what is said to have happened to the people of Shinak has precisely and practically happened to us.

None of us who have known Socialists (or rather, to speak more truthfully, none of us who have been Socialists) can entertain the faintest doubt that a fine intellectual sincerity lay behind what was called "L'Internationale." It was really felt that Socialism was universal like arithmetic. It was too true for idiom or turn of phrase. In the formula of Karl Marx men could find that frigid fellowship which they find when they agree that two and two make four. It was almost as broadminded as a religious dogma.

Yet this universal language has not succeeded, at a moment of crisis, in imposing itself on the whole world. Nay, it has not, at the moment of crisis, succeeded in imposing itself on its own principal champions. Herve is not talking Economic Esperanto; he is talking French. Bebel is not talking Economic Esperanto; he is talking German. Blatchford is not talking Economic Esperanto; he is talking English, and jolly good English, too. I do not know whether French or Flemish was Vandervelde's nursery speech, but I am quite certain he will know more of it after this struggle than he knew before. In short, whether or no there be a new union of hearts, there has really and truly been a new division of tongues.

How are we to explain this singular truth, even if we deplore it? I dismiss with fitting disdain the notion that it is a mere result of military terrorism or snobbish social pressure. The Socialist leaders of modern Europe are among the most sincere men in history; and their Nationalist note in this affair has had the ring of their sincerity. I will not waste time on the speculation that Vandervelde is bullied by Belgian priests; or that Blatchford is frightened of the horse-guards outside Whitehall. These great men support the enthusiasm of their conventional countrymen because they share it; and they share it because there is (though perhaps only at certain great moments) such a thing as pure democracy.

Timour the Tartar, I think, celebrated some victory with a tower built entirely out of human skulls; perhaps he thought *that* would reach to heaven. But there is no cement in such building; the veins and ligaments that hold humanity together have long fallen away; the skulls will roll impotently at a touch; and ten thousand more such trophies could only make the tower taller and crazier. I think the modern official apparatus of "votes" is very like that tottering monument. I think the Tartar "counted heads," like an electioneering agent. Sometimes when I have seen from the platform of some paltry party meeting the rows and rows of grinning upturned faces, I have felt inclined to say, as the poet does in the "The Vision of Sin"—"Welcome fellow-citizens, Hollow hearts and empty heads."

Not that the people were personally hollow or empty, but they had come on a hollow and empty business: to help the good Mr. Binks to strengthen the Insurance Act against the wicked Mr. Jinks who would only promise to fortify the Insurance Act. That night it did not blow the democratic gale. Yet it can blow on these as on others; and when it does blow men learn many things. I, for one, am not above learning them.

The Marxian dogma which simplifies all conflicts to the Class War is so much nobler a thing than the nose-counting of the parliaments that one must apologise for the comparison. And yet there is a comparison. When we used to say that there were so many thousands of Socialists in Germany, we were counting by skulls. When we said that the majority consisting of Proletarians would be everywhere opposed to the minority, consisting of Capitalists, we were counting by skulls. Why, yes; if all men's heads had been cut off from the rest of them, as they were by the good sense and foresight of Timour the Tartar; if they had no hearts or bellies to be moved; no hand that flies up to ward off a weapon, no foot that can feel a familiar soil—if things were so the Marxian calculation would be not only complete but correct. As we know to-day, the Marxian calculation is complete, but it is not correct.

Now, this is the answer to the questions of some kind critics, whose actual words I have not within reach at the moment, about whether my democracy meant the rule of the majority over the minority. It means the rule of the rule—the rule of the rule over the exception. When a nation finds a soul it clothes it with a body, and does verily act like one living thing. There is nothing to be said about those who are out of it, except that they are out of it. After talking about it in the abstract for decades, this is Democracy, and it is marvellous in our eyes. It is not the difference between ninety-nine persons and a hundred persons; it is one person—the people. I do not know or care how many or how few of the Belgians like or dislike the pictures of Wiertz. They could not be either justified or condemned by a mere majority of Belgians. But I am very certain that the defiance to Prussia did not come from a majority of Belgians. It came from Belgium one and indivisible—atheists, priests, princes of the blood, Frenchified shopkeepers, Flemish boors, men, women, and children, and the sooner we understand that this sort of thing can happen the better for us. For it is this spontaneous spiritual fellowship of communities under certain conditions to which the four or five most independent minds of Europe willingly bear witness to-day.

But is there no exception: is there no one faithful among the unfaithful found? Is no great Socialist politician still untouched by the patriotism of the vulgar? Why, yes; the rugged Ramsay MacDonald, scarred with a hundred savage fights against the capitalist parties, still lifts up his horny hand for peace. What further need have we of witnesses? I, for my part, am quite satisfied, and do not doubt that Mr. MacDonald will be as industrious in damping down democracy in this form as in every other.

A REAL DANGER

Heaven forbid that I should once more wade in those swamps of logomachy and tautology in which the old guard of the Determinists still seem to be floundering. The question of Fate and Free Will can never attain to a conclusion, though it may attain to a conviction. The shortest philosophic summary is that both cause and choice are ultimate ideas within us, and that if one man denies choice because it seems contrary to cause, the other man has quite as much right to deny cause because it seems contrary to choice. The shortest ethical summary is that Determinism either affects conduct or it does not. If it does not, it is morally not worth preaching; if it does, it must affect conduct in the direction of impotence and submission. A writer in the "Clarion" says that the reformer cannot help trying to reform, nor the Conservative help his Conservatism. But suppose the reformer tries to reform the Conservative and turn him into another reformer? Either he can, in which case Determinism has made no difference at all, or he can't, in which case it can only have made reformers more hopeless and Conservatives more obstinate. And the shortest practical and political summary is that working men, most probably, will soon be much too busy using their Free Will to stop to prove that they have got it. Nevertheless, I like to watch the Determinist in the "Clarion" Cockpit every week, as busy as a squirrel—in a cage. But being myself a squirrel (leaping lightly from bough to bough) and preferring the form of activity which occasionally ends in nuts, I should not intervene in the matter even indirectly, except upon a practical point. And the point I have in mind is practical to the extent of deadly peril. It is another of the numerous new ways in which the restless rich, now walking the world with an awful insomnia, may manage to catch us napping.

Must Be a Mystery

There are two letters in the "Clarion" this week which in various ways interest me very much. One is concerned to defend Darwin against the scientific revolt against him that was led by Samuel Butler, and among other things it calls Bernard Shaw a back number. Well, most certainly "The Origin of Species" is a back number, in so far as any honest and interesting book ever can be; but in pure philosophy nothing can be out of date, since the universe must be a mystery even to the believer. There is, however, one condition of things in which I do call it relevant to describe somebody as behind the times. That is when the man in question, thinking of some state of affairs that has passed away, is really helping the very things he would like to hinder. The principles cannot alter, but the problems can. Thus, I should call a man behind the times who, in the year 1872, pleaded for the peaceful German peasants against the triumphant militarism of Napoleon. Or I should call a man out of date who, in the year 1892, wished for a stronger Navy to compete with the Navy of Holland, because it had once swept the sea and sailed up the Thames. And I certainly call a man or a movement out of date that, in the year 1914, when we few are fighting a giant machine, strengthened with all material wealth and worked with all the material sciences, thinks that our chief danger is from an excess of moral and religious responsibility. He reminds me of Mr. Snodgrass, who had the presence of mind to call out "Fire!" when Mr. Pickwick fell through the ice.

The other letter consists of the usual wiredrawn argument for fatalism. Man cannot imagine the universe being created, and therefore is "compelled by his reason" to think the universe without beginning or end, which (I may remark) he cannot imagine either. But the letter ends with something much more ominous than bad metaphysics. Here, in the middle of the "Clarion," in the centre of a clean and combative democratic sheet, I meet again my deplorable old acquaintance, the scientific criminologist. "The so-called evil-doer should not be punished for his acts, but restrained." In forty-eight hours I could probably get a petition to that effect signed by millionaires. A short time ago a Bill was introduced to hold irresponsible and "restrain" a whole new class of people, who were "incapable of managing their affairs with prudence." Read the supporters' names on the back of that Bill, and see what sort of democrats they were.

Now, clearing our heads of what is called popular science (which means going to sleep to a lullaby of long words), let us use our own brains a little, and ask ourselves what is the real difference between punishing a man and restraining him. The material difference may be any or none; for punishment may be very mild, and restraint may be very ruthless. The man, of course, must dislike one as much as the other, or it would not be necessary to restrain him at all. And I assure you he will get no great glow of comfort out of your calling him irresponsible after you have made him impotent. A man does not necessarily feel more free and easy in a straight waistcoat than in a stone cell. The moral difference is that a man can be punished for a crime because he is born a citizen; while he can be constrained because he is born a slave. But one arresting and tremendous difference towers over all these doubtful or arguable differences. There is one respect, vital to all our liberties and all our lives, in which the new restraint would be different from the old punishment. It is of this that the plutocrats will take advantage.

The Plain Difference

The perfectly plain difference is this. All punishment, even the most horrible, proceeds upon the assumption that the extent of the evil is known, and that a certain amount of expiation goes with it. Even if you hang the man, you cannot hang him twice. Even if you burn him, you cannot burn him for a month. And in the case of all ordinary imprisonments, the whole aim of free institutions from the beginning of the world has been to insist that a man shall be convicted of a definite crime and confined for a definite period. But the moment you admit this notion of medical restraint, you must in fairness admit that it may go on as long as the authorities choose to think (or say) that it ought to go on. The man's punishment refers to the past, which is supposed to have been investigated, and which, in some degree at least, has been investigated. But his restraint refers to the future, which his doctors, keepers, and wardens have yet to investigate. The simple result will be that, in the scientific Utopia of the "Clarion," men like Mann or Syme or Larkin will not be put in prison because of what they have done. They will be kept in prison because of what they might do. Indeed, the builders of the new tyranny have already come very near to avowing this scientific and futurist method. When the lawyers tried to stop the "Suffragette" from appearing at all, they practically said: "We do not know your next week's crime, because it isn't committed yet; but we are scientifically certain you have the criminal type. And by the sublime and unalterable laws of heredity, all your poor little papers will inherit it."

This is a purely practical question; and that is why I insist on it, even in such strenuous times. The writers on the "Clarion" have a perfect right to think Christianity is the foe of freedom, or even that the stupidity and tyranny of the present Government is due to the monkish mysticism of Lord Morley and Mr. John M. Robertson. They have a right to think the theory of Determinism as true as Calvin thought it. But I do not like seeing them walk straight into the enormous iron trap set open by the Capitalists, who find it convenient to make our law even more lawless than it is. The rich men want a scientist to write them a *lettre de cachet* as a doctor writes a prescription. And so they wish to seal up in a public gaol the scandals of a private asylum. Yes; the writers on the "Clarion" are indeed claiming irresponsibility for human beings. But it is the governments that will be irresponsible, not the governed.

But I will tell them one small secret in conclusion. There is nothing whatever wrong in the ancient and universal idea of Punishment—except that we are not punishing the right people.

THE DREGS OF PURITANISM

One peculiarity of the genuine kind of enemy of the people is that his slightest phrase is clamorous with all his sins. Pride, vain-glory, and hypocrisy seem present in his very grammar; in his very verbs or adverbs or prepositions, as well as in what he says, which is generally bad enough. Thus I see that a Nonconformist pastor in Bromley has been talking about the pathetic little presents of tobacco sent to the common soldiers. This is how he talks about it. He is reported as having said, "By the help of God, they wanted this cigarette business stopped." How one could write a volume on that sentence, a great thick volume called "The Decline of the English Middle Class." In taste, in style, in philosophy, in feeling, in political project, the horrors of it are as unfathomable as hell.

First, to begin with the trifle, note something slipshod and vague in the mere verbiage, typical of those who prefer a catchword to a creed. "This cigarette business" might mean anything. It might mean Messrs. Salmon and Gluckstein's business. But the pastor at Bromley will not interfere with that, for the indignation of his school of thought, even when it is sincere, always instinctively and unconsciously swerves aside from anything that is rich and powerful like the partners in a big business, and strikes instead something that is poor and nameless like the soldiers in a trench. Nor does the expression make clear who "they" are—whether the inhabitants of Britain or the inhabitants of Bromley, or the inhabitants of this one crazy tabernacle in Bromley; nor is it evident how it is going to be stopped or who is being asked to stop it. All these things are trifles compared to the more terrible offences of the phrase; but they are not without their social and historical interest. About the beginning of the nineteenth century the wealthy Puritan class, generally the class of the employers of labour, took a line of argument which was narrow, but not nonsensical. They saw the relation of rich and poor quite coldly as a contract, but they saw that a contract holds both ways. The Puritans of the middle class, in short, did in some sense start talking and thinking for themselves. They are still talking. They have long ago left off thinking. They talk about the loyalty of workmen to their employers, and God knows what rubbish; and the first small certainty about the reverend gentleman whose sentence I have quoted is that his brain stopped working as a clock stops, years and years ago.

Second, consider the quality of the religious literature! These people are always telling us that the English translated Bible is sufficient training for anyone in noble and appropriate diction; and so it is. Why, then, are they not trained? They are always telling us that Bunyan, the rude Midland tinker, is as much worth reading as Chaucer or Spenser; and so he is. Why, then, have they not read him? I cannot believe that anyone who had seen, even in a nightmare of the nursery, Apollyon straddling over the whole breadth of the way could really write like that about a cigarette. By the help of God, they wanted this cigarette business stopped. Therefore, with angels and archangels and the whole company of Heaven, with St. Michael, smiter of Satan and Captain of the Chivalry of God, with all the ardour of the seraphs and the flaming patience of the saints, we will have this cigarette business stopped. Where has all the tradition of the great religious literatures gone to that a man should come on such a bathos with such a bump?

Thirdly, of course, there is the lack of imaginative proportion, which rises into a sort of towering blasphemy. An enormous number of live young men are being hurt by shells, hurt by bullets, hurt by fever and hunger and horror of hope deferred; hurt by lance blades and sword blades and bayonet blades breaking into the bloody house of life. But Mr. Price (I think that's his name) is still anxious that they should not be hurt by cigarettes. That is the sort of maniacal isolation that can be found in the deserts of Bromley. That cigarettes are bad for the health is a very tenable opinion to which the minister is quite entitled. If he happens to think that the youth of Bromley smoke too many cigarettes, and that he has any influence in urging on them the unhealthiness of the habit, I should not blame him if he gave sermons or lectures about it (with magic-lantern slides), so long as it was in Bromley and about Bromley. Cigarettes may be bad for the health: bombs and bayonets and even barbed wire are not good for the health. I never met a doctor who recommended any of them. But the trouble with this sort of man is that he cannot adjust himself to the scale of things. He would do very good service if he would go among the rich aristocratic ladies and tell them not to take drugs in a chronic sense, as people take opium in China. But he would be doing very bad service if he were to go among the doctors and nurses on the field and tell them not to give drugs, as they give morphia in a hospital. But it is the whole hypothesis of war, it is its very nature and first principle, that the man in the trench is almost as much a suffering and abnormal person as the man in the hospital. Hit or unhit, conqueror or conquered, he is, by nature of the case, having less pleasure than is proper and natural to a man.

Fourth (for I need not dwell here on the mere diabolical idiocy that can regard beer or tobacco as in some way evil and unseemly in themselves), there is the most important element in this strange outbreak; at least, the most dangerous and the most important for us. There is that main feature in the degradation of the old middle class: the utter disappearance of its old appetite for liberty. Here there is no question of whether the men are to smoke cigarettes, or the women choose to send cigarettes, or even that the officers or doctors choose to allow cigarettes. The thing is to cease, and we may note one of the most recurrent ideas of the servile State: it is mentioned in the passive mood. It must be stopped, and we must not even ask who has stopped it!

THE TYRANNY OF BAD JOURNALISM

The amazing decision of the Government to employ methods quite alien to England, and rather belonging to the police of the Continent, probably arises from the appearance of papers which are lucid and fighting, like the papers of the Continent. The business may be put in many ways. But one way of putting it is simply to say that a monopoly of bad journalism is resisting the possibility of good journalism. Journalism is not the same thing as literature; but there is good and bad journalism, as there is good and bad literature, as there is good and bad football. For the last twenty years or so the plutocrats who govern England have allowed the English nothing but bad journalism. Very bad journalism, simply considered as journalism.

It always takes a considerable time to see the simple and central fact about anything. All sorts of things have been said about the modern Press, especially the Yellow Press; that it is Jingo or Philistine or sensational or wrongly inquisitive or vulgar or indecent or trivial; but none of these have anything really to do with the point.

The point about the Press is that it is not what it is called. It is not the "popular Press." It is not the public Press. It is not an organ of public opinion. It is a conspiracy of a very few millionaires, all sufficiently similar in type to agree on the limits of what this great nation (to which we belong) may know about itself and its friends and enemies. The ring is not quite complete; there are old-fashioned and honest papers: but it is sufficiently near to completion to produce on the ordinary purchaser of news the practical effects of a corner and a monopoly. He receives all his political information and all his political marching orders from what is by this time a sort of half-conscious secret society, with very few members, but a great deal of money.

This enormous and essential fact is concealed for us by a number of legends that have passed into common speech. There is the notion that the Press is flashy or trivial *because* it is popular. In other words, an attempt is made to discredit democracy by representing journalism as the natural literature of democracy. All this is cold rubbish. The democracy has no more to do with the papers than it has with the peerages. The millionaire newspapers are vulgar and silly because the millionaires are vulgar and silly. It is the proprietor, not the editor, not the sub-editor, least of all the reader, who is pleased with this monotonous prairie of printed words. The same slander on democracy can be noticed in the case of advertisements. There is many a tender old Tory imagination that vaguely feels that our streets would be hung with escutcheons and tapestries, if only the profane vulgar had not hung them with advertisements of Sapolio and Sunlight Soap. But advertisement does not come from the unlettered many. It comes from the refined few. Did you ever hear of a mob rising to placard the Town Hall with proclamations in favour of Sapolio? Did you ever see a poor, ragged man laboriously drawing and painting a picture on the wall in favour of Sunlight Soap—simply as a labour of love? It is nonsense; those who hang our public walls with ugly pictures are the same select few who hang their private walls with exquisite and expensive pictures. The vulgarisation of modern life has come from the governing class; from the highly educated class. Most of the people who have posters in Camberwell have peerages at Westminster. But the strongest instance of all is that which has been unbroken until lately, and still largely prevails; the ghastly monotony of the Press.

Then comes that other legend; the notion that men like the masters of the Newspaper Trusts "give the people what they want." Why, it is the whole aim and definition of a Trust that it gives the people what it chooses. In the old days, when Parliaments were free in England, it was discovered that one courtier was allowed to sell all the silk, and another to sell all the sweet wine. A member of the House of Commons humorously asked who was allowed to sell all the bread. I really tremble to think what that sarcastic legislator would have said if he had been put off with the modern nonsense about "gauging the public taste." Suppose the first courtier had said that, by his shrewd, self-made sense, he had detected that people had a vague desire for silk; and even a deep, dim human desire to pay so much a yard for it! Suppose the second courtier said that he had, by his own rugged intellect, discovered a general desire for wine: and that people bought his wine at his price—when they could buy no other! Suppose a third courtier had jumped up and said that people always bought his bread when they could get none anywhere else.

Well, that is a perfect parallel. "After bread, the need of the people is knowledge," said Danton. Knowledge is now a monopoly, and comes through to the citizens in thin and selected streams, exactly as bread might come through to a besieged city. Men must wish to know what is happening, whoever has the privilege of telling them. They must listen to the messenger, even if he is a liar. They must listen to the liar, even if he is a bore. The official journalist for some time past has been both a bore and a liar; but it was impossible until lately to neglect his sheets of news altogether. Lately the capitalist Press really has begun to be neglected; because its bad journalism was overpowering and appalling. Lately we have really begun to find out that capitalism cannot write, just as it cannot fight, or pray, or marry, or make a joke, or do any other stricken human thing. But this discovery has been quite recent. The capitalist newspaper was never actually unread until it was actually unreadable.

If you retain the servile superstition that the Press, as run by the capitalists, is popular (in any sense except that in which dirty water in a desert is popular), consider the case of the solemn articles in praise of the men who own newspapers—men of the type of Cadbury or Harmsworth, men of the type of the small club of millionaires. Did you ever hear a plain man in a tramcar or train talking about Carnegie's bright genial smile or Rothschild's simple, easy hospitality? Did you ever hear an ordinary citizen ask what was the opinion of Sir Joseph Lyons about the hopes and fears of this, our native land? These few small-minded men publish, papers to praise themselves. You could no more get an intelligent poor man to praise a millionaire's soul, except for hire, than you could get him to sell a millionaire's soap, except for hire. And I repeat that, though there are other aspects of the matter of the new plutocratic raid, one of the most important is mere journalistic jealousy. The Yellow Press is bad journalism: and wishes to stop the appearance of good journalism.

There is no average member of the public who would not prefer to have Lloyd George discussed as what he is, a Welshman of genius and ideals, strangely fascinated by bad fashion and bad finance, rather than discussed as what neither he nor anyone else ever was, a perfect democrat or an utterly detestable demagogue. There is no reader of a daily paper who would not feel more concern—and more respect—for Sir Rufus Isaacs as a man who has been a stockbroker, than as a man who happens to be Attorney-General. There is no man in the street who is not more interested in Lloyd George's investments than in his Land Campaign. There is no man in the street who could not understand (and like) Rufus Isaacs as a Jew better than he can possibly like him as a British statesman. There is no sane journalist alive who would say that the official account of Marconis would be better "copy" than the true account that such papers as this have dragged out. We have committed one crime against the newspaper proprietor which he will never forgive. We point out that his papers are dull. And we propose to print some papers that are interesting.

THE POETRY OF THE REVOLUTION

Everyone but a consistent and contented capitalist, who must be something pretty near to a Satanist, must rejoice at the spirit and success of the Battle of the Buses. But one thing about it which happens to please me particularly was that it was fought, in one aspect at least, on a point such as the plutocratic fool calls unpractical. It was fought about a symbol, a badge, a thing attended with no kind of practical results, like the flags for which men allow themselves to fall down dead, or the shrines for which men will walk some hundreds of miles from their homes. When a man has an eye for business, all that goes on on this earth in that style is simply invisible to him. But let us be charitable to the eye for business; the eye has been pretty well blacked this time.

But I wish to insist here that it is exactly what is called the unpractical part of the thing that is really the practical. The chief difference between men and the animals is that all men are artists; though the overwhelming majority of us are bad artists. As the old fable truly says, lions do not make statues; even the cunning of the fox can go no further than the accomplishment of leaving an exact model of the vulpine paw: and even that is an accomplishment which he wishes he hadn't got. There are Chryselephantine statues, but no purely elephantine ones. And, though we speak in a general way of an elephant trumpeting, it is only by human blandishments that he can be induced to play the drum. But man, savage or civilised, simple or complex always desires to see his own soul outside himself; in some material embodiment. He always wishes to point to a table in a temple, or a cloth on a stick, or a word on a scroll, or a badge on a coat, and say: "This is the best part of me. If need be, it shall be the rest of me that shall perish." This is the method which seems so unbusinesslike to the men with an eye to business. This is also the method by which battles are won.

The Symbolism of the Badge

The badge on a Trade Unionist's coat is a piece of poetry in the genuine, lucid, and logical sense in which Milton defined poetry (and he ought to know) when he said that it was simple, sensuous, and passionate. It is simple, because many understand the word "badge," who might not even understand the word "recognition." It is sensuous, because it is visible and tangible; it is incarnate, as all the good Gods have been; and it is passionate in this perfectly practical sense, which the man with an eye to business may some day learn more thoroughly than he likes, that there are men who will allow you to cross a word out in a theoretical document, but who will not allow you to pull a big button off their bodily clothing, merely because you have more money than they have. Now I think it is this sensuousness, this passion, and, above all, this simplicity that are most wanted in this promising revolt of our time. For this simplicity is perhaps the only thing in which the best type of recent revolutionists have failed. It has been our sorrow lately to salute the sunset of one of the very few clean and incorruptible careers in the most corruptible phase of Christendom. The death of Quelch naturally turns one's thoughts to those extreme Marxian theorists, who, whatever we may hold about their philosophy, have certainly held their honour like iron. And yet, even in this instant of instinctive reverence, I cannot feel that they were poetical enough, that is childish enough, to make a revolution. They had all the audacity needed for speaking to the despot; but not the simplicity needed for speaking to the democracy. They were always accused of being too bitter against the capitalist. But it always seemed to me that they were (quite unconsciously, of course) much too kind to him. They had a fatal habit of using long words, even on occasions when he might with propriety have been described in very short words. They called him a Capitalist when almost anybody in Christendom would have called him a cad. And "cad" is a word from the poetic vocabulary indicating rather a general and powerful reaction of the emotions than a status that could be defined in a work of economics. The capitalist, asleep in the sun, let such long words crawl all over him, like so many long, soft, furry caterpillars. Caterpillars cannot sting like wasps. And, in repeating that the old Marxians have been, perhaps, the best and bravest men of our time, I say also that they would have been better and braver still if they had never used a scientific word, and never read anything but fairy tales.

The Beastly Individualist

Suppose I go on to a ship, and the ship sinks almost immediately; but I (like the people in the Bab Ballads), by reason of my clinging to a mast, upon a desert island am eventually cast. Or rather, suppose I am not cast on it, but am kept bobbing about in the water, because the only man on the island is what some call an Individualist, and will not throw me a rope; though coils of rope of the most annoying elaboration and neatness are conspicuous beside him as he stands upon the shore. Now, it seems to me, that if, in my efforts to shout at this fellow-creature across the crashing breakers, I call his position the "insularistic position," and my position "the semi-amphibian position," much valuable time may be lost. I am not an amphibian. I am a drowning man. He is not an insularist, or an individualist. He is a beast. Or rather, he is worse than any beast can be. And if, instead of letting me drown, he makes me promise, while I am drowning, that if I come on shore it shall be as his bodily slave, having no human claims henceforward forever, then, by the whole theory and practice of capitalism, he becomes a capitalist, he also becomes a cad.

Now, the language of poetry is simpler than that of prose; as anyone can see who has read what the old-fashioned protestant used to call confidently "his" Bible. And, being simpler, it is also truer; and, being truer, it is also fiercer. And, for most of the infamies of our time, there is really nothing plain enough, except the plain language of poetry. Take, let us say, the ease of the recent railway disaster, and the acquittal of the capitalists' interest. It is not a scientific problem for us to investigate. It is a crime committed before our eyes; committed, perhaps, by blind men or maniacs, or men hypnotised, or men in some other ways unconscious; but committed in broad daylight, so that the corpse is bleeding on our door-step. Good lives were lost, because good lives do not pay; and bad coals do pay. It seems simply impossible to get any other meaning out of the matter except that. And, if in human history there be anything simple and anything horrible, it seems to have been present in this matter. If, even after some study and understanding of the old religious passions which were the resurrection of Europe, we cannot endure the extreme infamy of witches and heretics literally burned alive—well, the people in this affair were quite as literally burned alive. If, when we have really tried to extend our charity beyond the borders of personal sympathy, to all the complexities of class and creed, we still feel something insolent about the triumphant and acquitted man who is in the wrong, here the men who are in the wrong are triumphant and acquitted. It is no subject for science. It is a subject for poetry. But for poetry of a terrible sort.

IMPERIALISM, OR THE MISTAKE ABOUT MAN

I. THE CHARM OF JINGOISM

I have cast about widely to find a title for this section; and I confess that the word "Imperialism" is a clumsy version of my meaning. But no other word came nearer; "Militarism" would have been even more misleading, and "The Superman" makes nonsense of any discussion that he enters. Perhaps, upon the whole, the word "Caesarism" would have been better; but I desire a popular word; and Imperialism (as the reader will perceive) does cover for the most part the men and theories that I mean to discuss.

This small confusion is increased, however, by the fact that I do also disbelieve in Imperialism in its popular sense, as a mode or theory of the patriotic sentiment of this country. But popular Imperialism in England has very little to do with the sort of Caesarean Imperialism I wish to sketch. I differ from the Colonial idealism of Rhodes' and Kipling; but I do not think, as some of its opponents do, that it is an insolent creation of English harshness and rapacity. Imperialism, I think, is a fiction created, not by English hardness, but by English softness; nay, in a sense, even by English kindness.

The reasons for believing in Australia are mostly as sentimental as the most sentimental reasons for believing in heaven. New South Wales is quite literally regarded as a place where the wicked cease from troubling and the weary are at rest; that is, a paradise for uncles who have turned dishonest and for nephews who are born tired. British Columbia is in strict sense a fairyland, it is a world where a magic and irrational luck is supposed to attend the youngest sons. This strange optimism about the ends of the earth is an English weakness; but to show that it is not a coldness or a harshness it is quite sufficient to say that no one shared it more than that gigantic English sentimentalist—the great Charles Dickens. The end of "David Copperfield" is unreal not merely because it is an optimistic ending, but because it is an Imperialistic ending. The decorous British happiness planned out for David Copperfield and Agnes would be embarrassed by the perpetual presence of the hopeless tragedy of Emily, or the more hopeless farce of Micawber. Therefore, both Emily and Micawber are shipped off to a vague colony where changes come over them with no conceivable cause, except the climate. The tragic woman becomes contented and the comic man becomes responsible, solely as the result of a sea voyage and the first sight of a kangaroo.

To Imperialism in the light political sense, therefore, my only objection is that it is an illusion of comfort; that an Empire whose heart is failing should be specially proud of the extremities, is to me no more sublime a fact than that an old dandy whose brain is gone should still be proud of his legs. It consoles men for the evident ugliness and apathy of England with legends of fair youth and heroic strenuousness in distant continents and islands. A man can sit amid the squalor of Seven Dials and feel that life is innocent and godlike in the bush or on the veldt. Just so a man might sit in the squalor of Seven Dials and feel that life was innocent and godlike in Brixton and Surbiton. Brixton and Surbiton are "new"; they are expanding; they are "nearer to nature," in the sense that they have eaten up nature mile by mile. The only objection is the objection of fact. The young men of Brixton are not young giants. The lovers of Surbiton are not all pagan poets, singing with the sweet energy of the spring. Nor are the people of the Colonies when you meet them young giants or pagan poets. They are mostly Cockneys who have lost their last music of real things by getting out of the sound of Bow Bells.

Mr. Rudyard Kipling, a man of real though decadent genius, threw a theoretic glamour over them which is already fading. Mr. Kipling is, in a precise and rather startling sense, the exception that proves the rule. For he has imagination, of an oriental and cruel kind, but he has it, not because he grew up in a new country, but precisely because he grew up in the oldest country upon earth. He is rooted in a past—an Asiatic past. He might never have written "Kabul River" if he had been born in Melbourne.

I say frankly, therefore (lest there should be any air of evasion), that Imperialism in its common patriotic pretensions appears to me both weak and perilous. It is the attempt of a European country to create a kind of sham Europe which it can dominate, instead of the real Europe, which it can only share. It is a love of living with one's inferiors. The notion of restoring the Roman Empire by oneself and for oneself is a dream that has haunted every Christian nation in a different shape and in almost every shape as a snare. The Spanish are a consistent and conservative people; therefore they embodied that attempt at Empire in long and lingering dynasties. The French are a violent people, and therefore they twice conquered that Empire by violence of arms. The English are above all a poetical and optimistic people; and therefore their Empire is something vague and yet sympathetic, something distant and yet dear. But this dream of theirs of being powerful in the uttermost places, though a native weakness, is still a weakness in them; much more of a weakness than gold was to Spain or glory to Napoleon. If ever we were in collision with our real brothers and rivals we should leave all this fancy out of account. We should no more dream of pitting Australian armies against German than of pitting Tasmanian sculpture against French. I have thus explained, lest anyone should accuse me of concealing an unpopular attitude, why I do not believe in Imperialism as commonly understood. I think it not merely an occasional wrong to other peoples, but a continuous feebleness, a running sore, in my own. But it is also true that I have dwelt on this Imperialism that is an amiable delusion partly in order to show how different it is from the deeper, more sinister and yet more persuasive thing that I have been forced to call Imperialism for the convenience of this chapter. In order to get to the root of this evil and quite un-English Imperialism we must cast back and begin anew with a more general discussion of the first needs of human intercourse.

II. WISDOM AND THE WEATHER

It is admitted, one may hope, that common things are never commonplace. Birth is covered with curtains precisely because it is a staggering and monstrous prodigy. Death and first love, though they happen to everybody, can stop one's heart with the very thought of them. But while this is granted, something further may be claimed. It is not merely true that these universal things are strange; it is moreover true that they are subtle. In the last analysis most common things will be found to be highly complicated. Some men of science do indeed get over the difficulty by dealing only with the easy part of it: thus, they will call first love the instinct of sex, and the awe of death the instinct of self-preservation. But this is only getting over the difficulty of describing peacock green by calling it blue. There is blue in it. That there is a strong physical element in both romance and the Memento Mori makes them if possible more baffling than if they had been wholly intellectual. No man could say exactly how much his sexuality was colored by a clean love of beauty, or by the mere boyish itch for irrevocable adventures, like running away to sea. No man could say how far his animal dread of the end was mixed up with mystical traditions touching morals and religion. It is exactly because these things are animal, but not quite animal, that the dance of all the difficulties begins. The materialists analyze the easy part, deny the hard part and go home to their tea.

It is complete error to suppose that because a thing is vulgar therefore it is not refined; that is, subtle and hard to define. A drawing-room song of my youth which began "In the gloaming, O, my darling," was vulgar enough as a song; but the connection between human passion and the twilight is none the less an exquisite and even inscrutable thing. Or to take another obvious instance: the jokes about a mother-in-law are scarcely delicate, but the problem of a mother-in-law is extremely delicate. A mother-in-law is subtle because she is a thing like the twilight. She is a mystical blend of two inconsistent things—law and a mother. The caricatures misrepresent her; but they arise out of a real human enigma. "Comic Cuts" deals with the difficulty wrongly, but it would need George Meredith at his best to deal with the difficulty rightly. The nearest statement of the problem perhaps is this: it is not that a mother-in-law must be nasty, but that she must be very nice.

But it is best perhaps to take in illustration some daily custom we have all heard despised as vulgar or trite. Take, for the sake of argument, the custom of talking about the weather. Stevenson calls it "the very nadir and scoff of good conversationalists." Now there are very deep reasons for talking about the weather, reasons that are delicate as well as deep; they lie in layer upon layer of stratified sagacity. First of all it is a gesture of primeval worship. The sky must be invoked; and to begin everything with the weather is a sort of pagan way of beginning everything with prayer. Jones and Brown talk about the weather: but so do Milton and Shelley. Then it is an expression of that elementary idea in politeness—equality. For the very word politeness is only the Greek for citizenship. The word politeness is akin to the word policeman: a charming thought. Properly understood, the citizen should be more polite than the gentleman; perhaps the policeman should be the most courtly and elegant of the three. But all good manners must obviously begin with the sharing of something in a simple style. Two men should share an umbrella; if they have not got an umbrella, they should at least share the rain, with all its rich potentialities of wit and philosophy. "For He maketh His sun to shine...." This is the second element in the weather; its recognition of human equality in that we all have our hats under the dark blue spangled umbrella of the universe. Arising out of this is the third wholesome strain in the custom; I mean that it begins with the body and with our inevitable bodily brotherhood. All true friendliness begins with fire and food and drink and the recognition of rain or frost. Those who will not begin at the bodily end of things are already prigs and may soon be Christian Scientists. Each human soul has in a sense to enact for itself the gigantic humility of the Incarnation. Every man must descend into the flesh to meet mankind.

Briefly, in the mere observation "a fine day" there is the whole great human idea of comradeship. Now, pure comradeship is another of those broad and yet bewildering things. We all enjoy it; yet when we come to talk about it we almost always talk nonsense, chiefly because we suppose it to be a simpler affair than it is. It is simple to conduct; but it is by no means simple to analyze. Comradeship is at the most only one half of human life; the other half is Love, a thing so different that one might fancy it had been made for another universe. And I do not mean mere sex love; any kind of concentrated passion, maternal love, or even the fiercer kinds of friendship are in their nature alien to pure comradeship. Both sides are essential to life; and both are known in differing degrees to everybody of every age or sex. But very broadly speaking it may still be said that women stand for the dignity of love and men for the dignity of comradeship. I mean that the institution would hardly be expected if the males of the tribe did not mount guard over it. The affections in which women excel have so much more authority and intensity that pure comradeship would be washed away if it were not rallied and guarded in clubs, corps, colleges, banquets and regiments. Most of us have heard the voice in which the hostess tells her husband not to sit too long over the cigars. It is the dreadful voice of Love, seeking to destroy Comradeship.

All true comradeship has in it those three elements which I have remarked in the ordinary exclamation about the weather. First, it has a sort of broad philosophy like the common sky, emphasizing that we are all under the same cosmic conditions. We are all in the same boat, the "winged rock" of Mr. Herbert Trench. Secondly, it recognizes this bond as the essential one; for comradeship is simply humanity seen in that one aspect in which men are really equal. The old writers were entirely wise when they talked of the equality of men; but they were also very wise in not mentioning women. Women are always authoritarian; they are always above or below; that is why marriage is a sort of poetical see-saw. There are only three things in the world that women do not understand; and they are Liberty, Equality, and Fraternity. But men (a class little understood in the modern world) find these things the breath of their nostrils; and our most learned ladies will not even begin to understand them until they make allowance for this kind of cool camaraderie. Lastly, it contains the third quality of the weather, the insistence upon the body and its indispensable satisfaction. No one has even begun to understand comradeship who does not accept with it a certain hearty eagerness in eating, drinking, or smoking, an uproarious materialism which to many women appears only hoggish. You may call the thing an orgy or a sacrament; it is certainly an essential. It is at root a resistance to the superciliousness of the individual. Nay, its very swaggering and howling are humble. In the heart of its rowdiness there is a sort of mad modesty; a desire to melt the separate soul into the mass of unpretentious masculinity. It is a clamorous confession of the weakness of all flesh. No man must be superior to the things that are common to men. This sort of equality must be bodily and gross and comic. Not only are we all in the same boat, but we are all seasick.

The word comradeship just now promises to become as fatuous as the word "affinity." There are clubs of a Socialist sort where all the members, men and women, call each other "Comrade." I have no serious emotions, hostile or otherwise, about this particular habit: at the worst it is conventionality, and at the best flirtation. I am convinced here only to point out a rational principle. If you choose to lump all flowers together, lilies and dahlias and tulips and chrysanthemums and call them all daisies, you will find that you have spoiled the very fine word daisy. If you choose to call every human attachment comradeship, if you include under that name the respect of a youth for a venerable prophetess, the interest of a man in a beautiful woman who baffles him, the pleasure of a philosophical old fogy in a girl who is impudent and innocent, the end of the meanest quarrel or the beginning of the most mountainous love; if you are going to call all these comradeship, you will gain nothing, you will only lose a word. Daisies are obvious and universal and open; but they are only one kind of flower. Comradeship is obvious and universal and open; but it is only one kind of affection; it has characteristics that would destroy any other kind. Anyone who has known true comradeship in a club or in a regiment, knows that it is impersonal. There is a pedantic phrase used in debating clubs which is strictly true to the masculine emotion; they call it "speaking to the question." Women speak to each other; men speak to the subject they are speaking about. Many an honest man has sat in a ring of his five best friends under heaven and forgotten who was in the room while he explained some system. This is not peculiar to intellectual men; men are all theoretical, whether they are talking about God or about golf. Men are all impersonal; that is to say, republican. No one remembers after a really good talk who has said the good things. Every man speaks to a visionary multitude; a mystical cloud, that is called the club.

It is obvious that this cool and careless quality which is essential to the collective affection of males involves disadvantages and dangers. It leads to spitting; it leads to coarse speech; it must lead to these things so long as it is honorable; comradeship must be in some degree ugly. The moment beauty is mentioned in male friendship, the nostrils are stopped with the smell of abominable things. Friendship must be physically dirty if it is to be morally clean. It must be in its shirt sleeves. The chaos of habits that always goes with males when left entirely to themselves has only one honorable cure; and that is the strict discipline of a monastery. Anyone who has seen our unhappy young idealists in East End Settlements losing their collars in the wash and living on tinned salmon will fully understand why it was decided by the wisdom of St. Bernard or St. Benedict, that if men were to live without women, they must not live without rules. Something of the same sort of artificial exactitude, of course, is obtained in an army; and an army also has to be in many ways monastic; only that it has celibacy without chastity. But these things do not apply to normal married men. These have a quite sufficient restraint on their instinctive anarchy in the savage common-sense of the other sex. There is only one very timid sort of man that is not afraid of women.

III. THE COMMON VISION

Now this masculine love of an open and level camaraderie is the life within all democracies and attempts to govern by debate; without it the republic would be a dead formula. Even as it is, of course, the spirit of democracy frequently differs widely from the letter, and a pothouse is often a better test than a Parliament. Democracy in its human sense is not arbitrament by the majority; it is not even arbitrament by everybody. It can be more nearly defined as arbitrament by anybody. I mean that it rests on that club habit of taking a total stranger for granted, of assuming certain things to be inevitably common to yourself and him. Only the things that anybody may be presumed to hold have the full authority of democracy. Look out of the window and notice the first man who walks by. The Liberals may have swept England with an over-whelming majority; but you would not stake a button that the man is a Liberal. The Bible may be read in all schools and respected in all law courts; but you would not bet a straw that he believes in the Bible. But you would bet your week's wages, let us say, that he believes in wearing clothes. You would bet that he believes that physical courage is a fine thing, or that parents have authority over children. Of course, he might be the millionth man who does not believe these things; if it comes to that, he might be the Bearded Lady dressed up as a man. But these prodigies are quite a different thing from any mere calculation of numbers. People who hold these views are not a minority, but a monstrosity. But of these universal dogmas that have full democratic authority the only test is this test of anybody. What you would observe before any newcomer in a tavern—that is the real English law. The first man you see from the window, he is the King of England.

The decay of taverns, which is but a part of the general decay of democracy, has undoubtedly weakened this masculine spirit of equality.

I remember that a roomful of Socialists literally laughed when I told them that there were no two nobler words in all poetry than Public House. They thought it was a joke. Why they should think it a joke, since they want to make all houses public houses, I cannot imagine. But if anyone wishes to see the real rowdy egalitarianism which is necessary (to males, at least) he can find it as well as anywhere in the great old tavern disputes which come down to us in such books as Boswell's Johnson. It is worth while to mention that one name especially because the modern world in its morbidity has done it a strange injustice. The demeanor of Johnson, it is said, was "harsh and despotic." It was occasionally harsh, but it was never despotic. Johnson was not in the least a despot; Johnson was a demagogue, he shouted against a shouting crowd. The very fact that he wrangled with other people is proof that other people were allowed to wrangle with him. His very brutality was based on the idea of an equal scrimmage, like that of football. It is strictly true that he bawled and banged the table because he was a modest man. He was honestly afraid of being overwhelmed or even overlooked. Addison had exquisite manners and was the king of his company; he was polite to everybody; but superior to everybody; therefore he has been handed down forever in the immortal insult of Pope—

"Like Cato, give his little Senate laws And sit attentive to his own applause."

Johnson, so far from being king of his company, was a sort of Irish Member in his own Parliament. Addison was a courteous superior and was hated. Johnson was an insolent equal and therefore was loved by all who knew him, and handed down in a marvellous book, which is one of the mere miracles of love.

This doctrine of equality is essential to conversation; so much may be admitted by anyone who knows what conversation is. Once arguing at a table in a tavern the most famous man on earth would wish to be obscure, so that his brilliant remarks might blaze like the stars on the background of his obscurity. To anything worth calling a man nothing can be conceived more cold or cheerless than to be king of your company. But it may be said that in masculine sports and games, other than the great game of debate, there is definite emulation and eclipse. There is indeed emulation, but this is only an ardent sort of equality. Games are competitive, because that is the only way of making them exciting. But if anyone doubts that men must forever return to the ideal of equality, it is only necessary to answer that there is such a thing as a handicap. If men exulted in mere superiority, they would seek to see how far such superiority could go; they would be glad when one strong runner came in miles ahead of all the rest. But what men like is not the triumph of superiors, but the struggle of equals; and, therefore, they introduce even into their competitive sports an artificial equality. It is sad to think how few of those who arrange our sporting handicaps can be supposed with any probability to realize that they are abstract and even severe republicans.

No; the real objection to equality and self-rule has nothing to do with any of these free and festive aspects of mankind; all men are democrats when they are happy. The philosophic opponent of democracy would substantially sum up his position by saying that it "will not work." Before going further, I will register in passing a protest against the assumption that working is the one test of humanity. Heaven does not work; it plays. Men are most themselves when they are free; and if I find that men are snobs in their work but democrats on their holidays, I shall take the liberty to believe their holidays. But it is this question of work which really perplexes the question of equality;

and it is with that that we must now deal. Perhaps the truth can be put most pointedly thus: that democracy has one real enemy, and that is civilization. Those utilitarian miracles which science has made are anti-democratic, not so much in their perversion, or even in their practical result, as in their primary shape and purpose. The Frame-Breaking Rioters were right; not perhaps in thinking that machines would make fewer men workmen; but certainly in thinking that machines would make fewer men masters. More wheels do mean fewer handles; fewer handles do mean fewer hands. The machinery of science must be individualistic and isolated. A mob can shout round a palace; but a mob cannot shout down a telephone. The specialist appears and democracy is half spoiled at a stroke.

IV. THE INSANE NECESSITY

The common conception among the dregs of Darwinian culture is that men have slowly worked their way out of inequality into a state of comparative equality. The truth is, I fancy, almost exactly the opposite. All men have normally and naturally begun with the idea of equality; they have only abandoned it late and reluctantly, and always for some material reason of detail. They have never naturally felt that one class of men was superior to another; they have always been driven to assume it through certain practical limitations of space and time.

For example, there is one element which must always tend to oligarchy—or rather to despotism; I mean the element of hurry. If the house has caught fire a man must ring up the fire engines; a committee cannot ring them up. If a camp is surprised by night somebody must give the order to fire; there is no time to vote it. It is solely a question of the physical limitations of time and space; not at all of any mental limitations in the mass of men commanded. If all the people in the house were men of destiny it would still be better that they should not all talk into the telephone at once; nay, it would be better that the silliest man of all should speak uninterrupted. If an army actually consisted of nothing but Hanibals and Napoleons, it would still be better in the case of a surprise that they should not all give orders together. Nay, it would be better if the stupidest of them all gave the orders. Thus, we see that merely military subordination, so far from resting on the inequality of men, actually rests on the equality of men. Discipline does not involve the Carlylean notion that somebody is always right when everybody is wrong, and that we must discover and crown that somebody. On the contrary, discipline means that in certain frightfully rapid circumstances, one can trust anybody so long as he is not everybody. The military spirit does not mean (as Carlyle fancied) obeying the strongest and wisest man. On the contrary, the military spirit means, if anything, obeying the weakest and stupidest man, obeying him merely because he is a man, and not a thousand men. Submission to a weak man is discipline. Submission to a strong man is only servility.

Now it can be easily shown that the thing we call aristocracy in Europe is not in its origin and spirit an aristocracy at all. It is not a system of spiritual degrees and distinctions like, for example, the caste system of India, or even like the old Greek distinction between free men and slaves. It is simply the remains of a military organization, framed partly to sustain the sinking Roman Empire, partly to break and avenge the awful onslaught of Islam. The word Duke simply means Colonel, just as the word Emperor simply means Commander-in-Chief. The whole story is told in the single title of Counts of the Holy Roman Empire, which merely means officers in the European army against the contemporary Yellow Peril. Now in an army nobody ever dreams of supposing that difference of rank represents a difference of moral reality. Nobody ever says about a regiment, "Your Major is very humorous and energetic; your Colonel, of course, must be even more humorous and yet more energetic." No one ever says, in reporting a mess-room conversation, "Lieutenant Jones was very witty, but was naturally inferior to Captain Smith." The essence of an army is the idea of official inequality, founded on unofficial equality. The Colonel is not obeyed because he is the best man, but because he is the Colonel. Such was probably the spirit of the system of dukes and counts when it first arose out of the military spirit and military necessities of Rome. With the decline of those necessities it has gradually ceased to have meaning as a military organization, and become honeycombed with unclean plutocracy. Even now it is not a spiritual aristocracy—it is not so bad as all that. It is simply an army without an enemy—billeted upon the people.

Man, therefore, has a specialist as well as comrade-like aspect; and the case of militarism is not the only case of such specialist submission. The tinker and tailor, as well as the soldier and sailor, require a certain rigidity of rapidity of action: at least, if the tinker is not organized that is largely why he does not tink on any large scale. The tinker and tailor often represent the two nomadic races in Europe: the Gipsy and the Jew; but the Jew alone has influence because he alone accepts some sort of discipline. Man, we say, has two sides, the specialist side where he must have subordination, and the social side where he must have equality. There is a truth in the saying that ten tailors go to make a man; but we must remember also that ten Poets Laureate or ten Astronomers Royal go to make a man, too. Ten million tradesmen go to make Man himself; but humanity consists of tradesmen when they are not talking shop. Now the peculiar peril of our time, which I call for argument's sake Imperialism or Caesarism, is the complete eclipse of comradeship and equality by specialism and domination.

There are only two kinds of social structure conceivable—personal government and impersonal government. If my anarchic friends will not have rules—they will have rulers. Preferring personal government, with its tact and flexibility, is called Royalism. Preferring impersonal government, with its dogmas and definitions, is called Republicanism. Objecting broadmindedly both to kings and creeds is called Bosh; at least, I know no more philosophic word for it. You can be guided by the shrewdness or presence of mind of one ruler, or by the equality and ascertained justice of one rule; but you must have one or the other, or you are not a nation, but a nasty mess. Now men in their aspect of equality and debate adore the idea of rules; they develop and complicate them greatly to excess. A man finds far more regulations and definitions in his club, where there are rules, than in his home, where there is a ruler. A deliberate assembly, the House of Commons, for instance, carries this mummery to the point of a methodical madness. The whole system is stiff with rigid unreason; like the Royal Court in Lewis Carroll. You would think the Speaker would speak; therefore he is mostly silent. You would think a man would take off his hat to stop and put it on to go away; therefore he takes off his hat to walk out and puts it on to stop in. Names are forbidden, and a man must call his own father "my right honorable friend the member for West Birmingham." These are, perhaps, fantasies of decay: but fundamentally they answer a masculine appetite. Men feel that rules, even if irrational, are universal; men feel that law is equal, even when it is not equitable. There is a wild fairness in the thing—as there is in tossing up.

Again, it is gravely unfortunate that when critics do attack such cases as the Commons it is always on the points (perhaps the few points) where the Commons are right. They denounce the House as the Talking-Shop, and complain that it wastes time in wordy mazes. Now this is just one respect in which the Commons are actually like the

Common People. If they love leisure and long debate, it is because all men love it; that they really represent England. There the Parliament does approach to the virile virtues of the pothouse.

The real truth is that adumbrated in the introductory section when we spoke of the sense of home and property, as now we speak of the sense of counsel and community. All men do naturally love the idea of leisure, laughter, loud and equal argument; but there stands a specter in our hall. We are conscious of the towering modern challenge that is called specialism or cut-throat competition—Business. Business will have nothing to do with leisure; business will have no truck with comradeship; business will pretend to no patience with all the legal fictions and fantastic handicaps by which comradeship protects its egalitarian ideal. The modern millionaire, when engaged in the agreeable and typical task of sacking his own father, will certainly not refer to him as the right honorable clerk from the Laburnum Road, Brixton. Therefore there has arisen in modern life a literary fashion devoting itself to the romance of business, to great demigods of greed and to fairyland of finance. This popular philosophy is utterly despotic and anti-democratic; this fashion is the flower of that Caesarism against which I am concerned to protest. The ideal millionaire is strong in the possession of a brain of steel. The fact that the real millionaire is rather more often strong in the possession of a head of wood, does not alter the spirit and trend of the idolatry. The essential argument is "Specialists must be despots; men must be specialists. You cannot have equality in a soap factory; so you cannot have it anywhere. You cannot have comradeship in a wheat corner; so you cannot have it at all. We must have commercial civilization; therefore we must destroy democracy." I know that plutocrats have seldom sufficient fancy to soar to such examples as soap or wheat. They generally confine themselves, with fine freshness of mind, to a comparison between the state and a ship. One anti-democratic writer remarked that he would not like to sail in a vessel in which the cabin-boy had an equal vote with the captain. It might easily be urged in answer that many a ship (the Victoria, for instance) was sunk because an admiral gave an order which a cabin-boy could see was wrong. But this is a debating reply; the essential fallacy is both deeper and simpler. The elementary fact is that we were all born in a state; we were not all born on a ship; like some of our great British bankers. A ship still remains a specialist experiment, like a diving-bell or a flying ship: in such peculiar perils the need for promptitude constitutes the need for autocracy. But we live and die in the vessel of the state; and if we cannot find freedom camaraderie and the popular element in the state, we cannot find it at all. And the modern doctrine of commercial despotism means that we shall not find it at all. Our specialist trades in their highly civilized state cannot (it says) be run without the whole brutal business of bossing and sacking, "too old at forty" and all the rest of the filth. And they must be run, and therefore we call on Caesar. Nobody but the Superman could descend to do such dirty work.

Now (to reiterate my title) this is what is wrong. This is the huge modern heresy of altering the human soul to fit its conditions, instead of altering human conditions to fit the human soul. If soap boiling is really inconsistent with brotherhood, so much the worst for soap-boiling, not for brotherhood. If civilization really cannot get on with democracy, so much the worse for civilization, not for democracy. Certainly, it would be far better to go back to village communes, if they really are communes. Certainly, it would be better to do without soap rather than to do without society. Certainly, we would sacrifice all our wires, wheels, systems, specialties, physical science and frenzied finance for one half-hour of happiness such as has often come to us with comrades in a common tavern. I do not say the sacrifice will be necessary; I only say it will be easy.

THE HOME OF MAN

I. THE EMPIRE OF THE INSECT

A cultivated Conservative friend of mine once exhibited great distress because in a gay moment I once called Edmund Burke an atheist. I need scarcely say that the remark lacked something of biographical precision; it was meant to. Burke was certainly not an atheist in his conscious cosmic theory, though he had not a special and flaming faith in God, like Robespierre. Nevertheless, the remark had reference to a truth which it is here relevant to repeat. I mean that in the quarrel over the French Revolution, Burke did stand for the atheistic attitude and mode of argument, as Robespierre stood for the theistic. The Revolution appealed to the idea of an abstract and eternal justice, beyond all local custom or convenience. If there are commands of God, then there must be rights of man. Here Burke made his brilliant diversion; he did not attack the Robespierre doctrine with the old mediaeval doctrine of jus divinum (which, like the Robespierre doctrine, was theistic), he attacked it with the modern argument of scientific relativity; in short, the argument of evolution. He suggested that humanity was everywhere molded by or fitted to its environment and institutions; in fact, that each people practically got, not only the tyrant it deserved, but the tyrant it ought to have. "I know nothing of the rights of men," he said, "but I know something of the rights of Englishmen." There you have the essential atheist. His argument is that we have got some protection by natural accident and growth; and why should we profess to think beyond it, for all the world as if we were the images of God! We are born under a House of Lords, as birds under a house of leaves; we live under a monarchy as niggers live under a tropic sun; it is not their fault if they are slaves, and it is not ours if we are snobs. Thus, long before Darwin struck his great blow at democracy, the essential of the

Darwinian argument had been already urged against the French Revolution. Man, said Burke in effect, must adapt himself to everything, like an animal; he must not try to alter everything, like an angel. The last weak cry of the pious, pretty, half-artificial optimism and deism of the eighteenth century came in the voice of Sterne, saying, "God tempers the wind to the shorn lamb." And Burke, the iron evolutionist, essentially answered, "No; God tempers the shorn lamb to the wind." It is the lamb that has to adapt himself. That is, he either dies or becomes a particular kind of lamb who likes standing in a draught.

The subconscious popular instinct against Darwinism was not a mere offense at the grotesque notion of visiting one's grandfather in a cage in the Regent's Park. Men go in for drink, practical jokes and many other grotesque things; they do not much mind making beasts of themselves, and would not much mind having beasts made of their forefathers. The real instinct was much deeper and much more valuable. It was this: that when once one begins to think of man as a shifting and alterable thing, it is always easy for the strong and crafty to twist him into new shapes for all kinds of unnatural purposes. The popular instinct sees in such developments the possibility of backs bowed and hunch-backed for their burden, or limbs twisted for their task. It has a very well-grounded guess that whatever is done swiftly and systematically will mostly be done by a successful class and almost solely in their interests. It has therefore a vision of inhuman hybrids and half-human experiments much in the style of Mr. Wells's "Island of Dr. Moreau." The rich man may come to breeding a tribe of dwarfs to be his jockeys, and a tribe of giants to be his hall-porters. Grooms might be born bow-legged and tailors born cross-legged; perfumers might have long, large noses and a crouching attitude, like hounds of scent; and professional wine-tasters might have the horrible expression of one tasting wine stamped upon their faces as infants. Whatever wild image one employs it cannot keep pace with the panic of the human fancy, when once it supposes that the fixed type called man could be changed. If some millionaire wanted arms, some porter must grow ten arms like an octopus; if he wants legs, some messenger-boy must go with a hundred trotting legs like a centipede. In the distorted mirror of hypothesis, that is, of the unknown, men can dimly see such monstrous and evil shapes; men run all to eye, or all to fingers, with nothing left but one nostril or one ear. That is the nightmare with which the mere notion of adaptation threatens us. That is the nightmare that is not so very far from the reality.

It will be said that not the wildest evolutionist really asks that we should become in any way unhuman or copy any other animal. Pardon me, that is exactly what not merely the wildest evolutionists urge, but some of the tamest evolutionists too. There has risen high in recent history an important cultus which bids fair to be the religion of the future—which means the religion of those few weak-minded people who live in the future. It is typical of our time that it has to look for its god through a microscope; and our time has marked a definite adoration of the insect. Like most things we call new, of course, it is not at all new as an idea; it is only new as an idolatry. Virgil takes bees seriously but I doubt if he would have kept bees as carefully as he wrote about them. The wise king told the sluggard to watch the ant, a charming occupation —for a sluggard. But in our own time has appeared a very different tone, and more than one great man, as well as numberless intelligent men, have in our time seriously suggested that we should study the insect because we are his inferiors. The old moralists merely took the virtues of man and distributed them quite decoratively and arbitrarily among the animals. The ant was an almost heraldic symbol of industry, as the lion was of courage, or, for the matter of that, the pelican of charity. But if the mediaevals had been convinced that a lion was not courageous, they would have dropped the lion and kept the courage; if the pelican is not charitable, they would say, so much the worse for the pelican. The old moralists, I say, permitted the ant to enforce and typify man's morality; they never allowed the ant to upset it. They used the ant for industry as the lark for punctuality; they looked up at the flapping birds and down at the crawling insects for a homely lesson. But we have lived to see a sect that does not look down at the insects, but looks up at the insects, that asks us essentially to bow down and worship beetles, like ancient Egyptians.

Maurice Maeterlinck is a man of unmistakable genius, and genius always carries a magnifying glass. In the terrible crystal of his lens we have seen the bees not as a little yellow swarm, but rather in golden armies and hierarchies of warriors and queens. Imagination perpetually peers and creeps further down the avenues and vistas in the tubes of science, and one fancies every frantic reversal of proportions; the earwig striding across the echoing plain like an elephant, or the grasshopper coming roaring above our roofs like a vast aeroplane, as he leaps from Hertfordshire to Surrey. One seems to enter in a dream a temple of enormous entomology, whose architecture is based on something wilder than arms or backbones; in which the ribbed columns have the half-crawling look of dim and monstrous caterpillars; or the dome is a starry spider hung horribly in the void. There is one of the modern works of engineering that gives one something of this nameless fear of the exaggerations of an underworld; and that is the curious curved architecture of the under ground railway, commonly called the Twopenny Tube. Those squat archways, without any upright line or pillar, look as if they had been tunneled by huge worms who have never learned to lift their heads. It is the very underground palace of the Serpent, the spirit of changing shape and color, that is the enemy of man.

But it is not merely by such strange aesthetic suggestions that writers like Maeterlinck have influenced us in the matter; there is also an ethical side to the business. The upshot of M. Maeterlinck's book on bees is an admiration, one might also say an envy, of their collective spirituality; of the fact that they live only for something which he calls the Soul of the Hive. And this admiration for the communal morality of insects is expressed in many other modern writers in various quarters and shapes; in Mr. Benjamin Kidd's theory of living only for the evolutionary future of our race, and in the great interest of some Socialists in ants, which they generally prefer to bees, I suppose, because they are not so brightly colored. Not least among the hundred evidences of this vague insectolatry are the floods of flattery poured by modern people on that energetic nation of the Far East of which it has been said that "Patriotism is its only religion"; or, in other words, that it lives only for the Soul of the Hive. When at long intervals of the centuries Christendom grows weak, morbid or skeptical, and mysterious Asia begins to move against us her dim populations and to pour them westward like a dark movement of matter, in such cases it has been very common to compare the invasion to a plague of lice or incessant armies of locusts. The Eastern armies were indeed like insects; in their blind, busy destructiveness, in their black nihilism of personal outlook, in their hateful indifference to individual life and love, in their base belief in mere numbers, in their pessimistic courage and their atheistic patriotism, the riders and raiders of the East are indeed like all the creeping things of the earth. But never before, I think, have Christians called a Turk a locust and meant it as a compliment. Now for the first time we worship as well as fear; and trace with adoration that enormous form advancing vast and vague out of Asia, faintly discernible amid the mystic clouds of winged creatures hung over the wasted lands, thronging the skies like thunder and discoloring the skies like rain; Beelzebub, the Lord of Flies.

In resisting this horrible theory of the Soul of the Hive, we of Christendom stand not for ourselves, but for all humanity; for the essential and distinctive human idea that one good and happy man is an end in himself, that a soul is worth saving. Nay, for those who like such biological fancies it might well be said that we stand as chiefs and champions of a whole section of nature, princes of the house whose cognizance is the backbone, standing for the milk of the individual mother and the courage of the wandering cub, representing the pathetic chivalry of the dog, the humor and perversity of cats, the affection of the tranquil horse, the loneliness of the lion. It is more to the point, however, to urge that this mere glorification of society as it is in the social insects is a transformation and a dissolution in one of the outlines which have been specially the symbols of man. In the cloud and confusion of the flies and bees is growing fainter and fainter, as is finally disappearing, the idea of the human family. The hive has become larger than the house, the bees are destroying their captors; what the locust hath left, the caterpillar hath eaten; and the little house and garden of our friend Jones is in a bad way.

II. THE FALLACY OF THE UMBRELLA STAND

When Lord Morley said that the House of Lords must be either mended or ended, he used a phrase which has caused some confusion; because it might seem to suggest that mending and ending are somewhat similar things. I wish specially to insist on the fact that mending and ending are opposite things. You mend a thing because you like it; you end a thing because you don't. To mend is to strengthen. I, for instance, disbelieve in oligarchy; so I would no more mend the House of Lords than I would mend a thumbscrew. On the other hand, I do believe in the family; therefore I would mend the family as I would mend a chair; and I will never deny for a moment that the modern family is a chair that wants mending. But here comes in the essential point about the mass of modern advanced sociologists. Here are two institutions that have always been fundamental with mankind, the family and the state. Anarchists, I believe, disbelieve in both. It is quite unfair to say that Socialists believe in the state, but do not believe in the family; thousands of Socialists believe more in the family than any Tory. But it is true to say that while anarchists would end both, Socialists are specially engaged in mending (that is, strengthening and renewing) the state; and they are not specially engaged in strengthening and renewing the family. They are not doing anything to define the functions of father, mother, and child, as such; they are not tightening the machine up again; they are not blackening in again the fading lines of the old drawing. With the state they are doing this; they are sharpening its machinery, they are blackening in its black dogmatic lines, they are making mere government in every way stronger and in some ways harsher than before. While they leave the home in ruins, they restore the hive, especially the stings. Indeed, some schemes of labor and Poor Law reform recently advanced by distinguished Socialists, amount to little more than putting the largest number of people in the despotic power of Mr. Bumble. Apparently, progress means being moved on—by the police.

The point it is my purpose to urge might perhaps be suggested thus: that Socialists and most social reformers of their color are vividly conscious of the line between the kind of things that belong to the state and the kind of things that belong to mere chaos or uncoercible nature; they may force children to go to school before the sun rises, but they will not try to force the sun to rise; they will not, like Canute, banish the sea, but only the sea-bathers. But inside the outline of the state their lines are confused, and entities melt into each other. They have no firm instinctive sense of one thing being in its nature private and another public, of one thing being necessarily bond and another free. That is why piece by piece, and quite silently, personal liberty is being stolen from Englishmen, as personal land has been silently stolen ever since the sixteenth century.

I can only put it sufficiently curtly in a careless simile. A Socialist means a man who thinks a walking-stick like an umbrella because they both go into the umbrella-stand. Yet they are as different as a battle-ax and a bootjack. The essential idea of an umbrella is breadth and protection. The essential idea of a stick is slenderness and, partly, attack. The stick is the sword, the umbrella is the shield, but it is a shield against another and more nameless enemy—the hostile but anonymous universe. More properly, therefore, the umbrella is the roof; it is a kind of collapsible house. But the vital difference goes far deeper than this; it branches off into two kingdoms of man's mind, with a chasm between. For the point is this: that the umbrella is a shield against an enemy so actual as to be a mere nuisance; whereas the stick is a sword against enemies so entirely imaginary as to be a pure pleasure. The stick is not merely a sword, but a court sword; it is a thing of purely ceremonial swagger. One cannot express the emotion in any way except by saying that a man feels more like a man with a stick in his hand, just as he feels more like a man with a sword at his side. But nobody ever had any swelling sentiments about an umbrella; it is a convenience, like a door scraper. An umbrella is a necessary evil. A walking-stick is a quite unnecessary good. This, I fancy, is the real explanation of the perpetual losing of umbrellas; one does not hear of people losing walking sticks. For a walking-stick is a pleasure, a piece of real personal property; it is missed even when it is not needed. When my right hand forgets its stick may it forget its cunning. But anybody may forget an umbrella, as anybody might forget a shed that he has stood up in out of the rain. Anybody can forget a necessary thing.

If I might pursue the figure of speech, I might briefly say that the whole Collectivist error consists in saying that because two men can share an umbrella, therefore two men can share a walking-stick. Umbrellas might possibly be replaced by some kind of common awnings covering certain streets from particular showers. But there is nothing but nonsense in the notion of swinging a communal stick; it is as if one spoke of twirling a communal mustache. It will be said that this is a frank fantasia and that no sociologists suggest such follies. Pardon me if they do. I will give a precise parallel to the case of confusion of sticks and umbrellas, a parallel from a perpetually reiterated suggestion of reform. At least sixty Socialists out of a hundred, when they have spoken of common laundries, will go on at once to speak of common kitchens. This is just as mechanical and unintelligent as the fanciful case I have quoted. Sticks and umbrellas are both stiff rods that go into holes in a stand in the hall. Kitchens and washhouses are both large rooms full of heat and damp and steam. But the soul and function of the two things are utterly opposite. There is only one way of washing a shirt; that is, there is only one right way. There is no taste and fancy in tattered shirts. Nobody says, "Tompkins likes five holes in his shirt, but I must say, give me the good old four holes." Nobody says, "This washerwoman rips up the left leg of my pyjamas; now if there is one thing I insist on it is the right leg ripped up." The ideal washing is simply to send a thing back washed. But it is by no means true that the ideal cooking is simply to send a thing back cooked. Cooking is an art; it has in it personality, and even perversity, for the definition of an art is that which must be personal and may be perverse. I know a man, not otherwise dainty, who cannot touch common sausages unless they are almost burned to a coal. He wants his sausages fried to rags, yet he does not insist on his shirts being boiled to rags. I do not say that such points of culinary delicacy are of high importance. I do not say that the communal ideal must give way to them. What I say is that the communal ideal is not conscious of their existence, and therefore goes wrong from the very start, mixing a wholly public thing with a highly individual one. Perhaps we ought to accept communal kitchens in the social crisis, just as we should accept communal cat's-meat in a siege. But the cultured Socialist, quite at his ease, by no means in a siege, talks about communal kitchens as if they were the same kind of thing as communal laundries. This shows at the start that he misunderstands human nature. It is as different as three men singing the same chorus from three men playing three tunes on the same piano.

III. THE DREADFUL DUTY OF GUDGE

In the quarrel earlier alluded to between the energetic Progressive and the obstinate Conservative (or, to talk a tenderer language, between Hudge and Gudge), the state of cross-purposes is at the present moment acute. The Tory says he wants to preserve family life in Cindertown; the Socialist very reasonably points out to him that in Cindertown at present there isn't any family life to preserve. But Hudge, the Socialist, in his turn, is highly vague and mysterious about whether he would preserve the family life if there were any; or whether he will try to restore it where it has disappeared. It is all very confusing. The Tory sometimes talks as if he wanted to tighten the domestic bonds that do not exist; the Socialist as if he wanted to loosen the bonds that do not bind anybody. The question we all want to ask of both of them is the original ideal question, "Do you want to keep the family at all?" If Hudge, the Socialist, does want the family he must be prepared for the natural restraints, distinctions and divisions of labor in the family. He must brace himself up to bear the idea of the woman having a preference for the private house and a man for the public house. He must manage to endure somehow the idea of a woman being womanly, which does not mean soft and yielding, but handy, thrifty, rather hard, and very humorous. He must confront without a quiver the notion of a child who shall be childish, that is, full of energy, but without an idea of independence; fundamentally as eager for authority as for information and butter-scotch. If a man, a woman and a child live together any more in free and sovereign households, these ancient relations will recur; and Hudge must put up with it. He can only avoid it by destroying the family, driving both sexes into sexless hives and hordes, and bringing up all children as the children of the state—like Oliver Twist. But if these stern words must be addressed to Hudge, neither shall Gudge escape a somewhat severe admonition. For the plain truth to be told pretty sharply to the Tory is this, that if he wants the family to remain, if he wants to be strong enough to resist the rending forces of our essentially savage commerce, he must make some very big sacrifices and try to equalize property. The overwhelming mass of the English people at this particular instant are simply too poor to be domestic. They are as domestic as they can manage; they are much more domestic than the governing class; but they cannot get what good there was originally meant to be in this institution, simply because they have not got enough money. The man ought to stand for a certain magnanimity, quite lawfully expressed in throwing money away: but if under given circumstances he can only do it by throwing the week's food away, then he is not magnanimous, but mean. The woman ought to stand for a certain wisdom which is well expressed in valuing things rightly and guarding money sensibly; but how is she to guard money if there is no money to guard? The child ought to look on his mother as a fountain of natural fun and poetry; but how can he unless the fountain, like other fountains, is allowed to play? What chance have any of these ancient arts and functions in a house so hideously topsy-turvy; a house where the woman is out working and the man isn't; and the child is forced by law to think his schoolmaster's requirements more important than his mother's? No, Gudge and his friends in the House of Lords and the Carlton Club must make up their minds on this matter, and that very quickly. If they are content to have England turned into a beehive and an ant-hill, decorated here and there with a few faded butterflies playing at an old game called domesticity in the intervals of the divorce court, then let them have their empire of insects; they will find plenty of Socialists who will give it to them. But if they want a domestic England, they must "shell out," as the phrase goes, to a vastly greater extent than any Radical politician has yet dared to suggest; they must endure burdens much heavier than the Budget and strokes much deadlier than the death duties; for the thing to be done is nothing more nor less than the distribution of the great fortunes and the great estates. We can now only avoid Socialism by a change as vast as Socialism. If we are to save property, we must distribute property, almost as sternly and sweepingly as did the French Revolution. If we are to preserve the family we must revolutionize the nation.

IV. A LAST INSTANCE

And now, as this book is drawing to a close, I will whisper in the reader's ear a horrible suspicion that has sometimes haunted me: the suspicion that Hudge and Gudge are secretly in partnership. That the quarrel they keep up in public is very much of a put-up job, and that the way in which they perpetually play into each other's hands is not an everlasting coincidence. Gudge, the plutocrat, wants an anarchic industrialism; Hudge, the idealist, provides him with lyric praises of anarchy. Gudge wants women-workers because they are cheaper; Hudge calls the woman's work "freedom to live her own life." Gudge wants steady and obedient workmen, Hudge preaches teetotalism—to workmen, not to Gudge—Gudge wants a tame and timid population who will never take arms against tyranny; Hudge proves from Tolstoi that nobody must take arms against anything. Gudge is naturally a healthy and well-washed gentleman; Hudge earnestly preaches the perfection of Gudge's washing to people who can't practice it. Above all, Gudge rules by a coarse and cruel system of sacking and sweating and bi-sexual toil which is totally inconsistent with the free family and which is bound to destroy it; therefore Hudge, stretching out his arms to the universe with a prophetic smile, tells us that the family is something that we shall soon gloriously outgrow.

I do not know whether the partnership of Hudge and Gudge is conscious or unconscious. I only know that between them they still keep the common man homeless. I only know I still meet Jones walking the streets in the gray twilight, looking sadly at the poles and barriers and low red goblin lanterns which still guard the house which is none the less his because he has never been in it.

V. CONCLUSION

Here, it may be said, my book ends just where it ought to begin. I have said that the strong centers of modern English property must swiftly or slowly be broken up, if even the idea of property is to remain among Englishmen. There are two ways in which it could be done, a cold administration by quite detached officials, which is called Collectivism, or a personal distribution, so as to produce what is called Peasant Proprietorship. I think the latter solution the finer and more fully human, because it makes each man as somebody blamed somebody for saying of the Pope, a sort of small god. A man on his own turf tastes eternity or, in other words, will give ten minutes more work than is required. But I believe I am justified in shutting the door on this vista of argument, instead of opening it. For this book is not designed to prove the case for Peasant Proprietorship, but to prove the case against modern sages who turn reform to a routine. The whole of this book has been a rambling and elaborate urging of one purely ethical fact. And if by any chance it should happen that there are still some who do not quite see what that point is, I will end with one plain parable, which is none the worse for being also a fact.

A little while ago certain doctors and other persons permitted by modern law to dictate to their shabbier fellow-citizens, sent out an order that all little girls should have their hair cut short. I mean, of course, all little girls whose parents were poor. Many very unhealthy habits are common among rich little girls, but it will be long before any doctors interfere forcibly with them. Now, the case for this particular interference was this, that the poor are pressed down from above into such stinking and suffocating underworlds of squalor, that poor people must not be allowed to have hair, because in their case it must mean lice in the hair. Therefore, the doctors propose to abolish the hair. It never seems to have occurred to them to abolish the lice. Yet it could be done. As is common in most modern discussions the unmentionable thing is the pivot of the whole discussion. It is obvious to any Christian man (that is, to any man with a free soul) that any coercion applied to a cabman's daughter ought, if possible, to be applied to a Cabinet Minister's daughter. I will not ask why the doctors do not, as a matter of fact apply their rule to a Cabinet Minister's daughter. I will not ask, because I know. They do not because they dare not. But what is the excuse they would urge, what is the plausible argument they would use, for thus cutting and clipping poor children and not rich? Their argument would be that the disease is more likely to be in the hair of poor people than of rich. And why? Because the poor children are forced (against all the instincts of the highly domestic working classes) to crowd together in close rooms under a wildly inefficient system of public instruction; and because in one out of the forty children there may be offense. And why? Because the poor man is so ground down by the great rents of the great ground landlords that his wife often has to work as well as he. Therefore she has no time to look after the children, therefore one in forty of them is dirty. Because the workingman has these two persons on top of him, the landlord sitting (literally) on his stomach, and the schoolmaster sitting (literally) on his head, the workingman must allow his little girl's hair, first to be neglected from poverty, next to be poisoned by promiscuity, and, lastly, to be abolished by hygiene. He, perhaps, was proud of his little girl's hair. But he does not count.

Upon this simple principle (or rather precedent) the sociological doctor drives gayly ahead. When a crapulous tyranny crushes men down into the dirt, so that their very hair is dirty, the scientific course is clear. It would be long and laborious to cut off the heads of the tyrants; it is easier to cut off the hair of the slaves. In the same way, if it should ever happen that poor children, screaming with toothache, disturbed any schoolmaster or artistic gentleman, it would be easy to pull out all the teeth of the poor; if their nails were disgustingly dirty, their nails could be plucked out; if their noses were indecently blown, their noses could be cut off. The appearance of our humbler fellow-citizen could be quite strikingly simplified before we had done with him. But all this is not a bit wilder than the brute fact that a doctor can walk into the house of a free man, whose daughter's hair may be as clean as spring flowers, and order him to cut it off. It never seems to strike these people that the lesson of lice in the slums is the wrongness of slums, not the wrongness of hair. Hair is, to say the least of it, a rooted thing. Its enemy (like the other insects and oriental armies of whom we have spoken) sweep upon us but seldom. In truth, it is only by eternal institutions like hair that we can test passing institutions like empires. If a house is so built as to knock a man's head off when he enters it, it is built wrong.

The mob can never rebel unless it is conservative, at least enough to have conserved some reasons for rebelling. It is the most awful thought in all our anarchy, that most of the ancient blows struck for freedom would not be struck at all to-day, because of the obscuration of the clean, popular customs from which they came. The insult that brought down the hammer of Wat Tyler might now be called a medical examination. That which Virginius loathed and avenged as foul slavery might now be praised as free love. The cruel taunt of Foulon, "Let them eat grass," might now be represented as the dying cry of an idealistic vegetarian. Those great scissors of science that would snip off the curls of the poor little school children are ceaselessly snapping closer and closer to cut off all the corners and fringes of the arts and honors of the poor. Soon they will be twisting necks to suit clean collars, and hacking feet to fit new boots. It never seems to strike them that the body is more than raiment; that the Sabbath was made for man; that all institutions shall be judged and damned by whether they have fitted the normal flesh and spirit. It is the test of political sanity to keep your head. It is the test of artistic sanity to keep your hair on.

Now the whole parable and purpose of these last pages, and indeed of all these pages, is this: to assert that we must instantly begin all over again, and begin at the other end. I begin with a little girl's hair. That I know is a good thing at any rate. Whatever else is evil, the pride of a good mother in the beauty of her daughter is good. It is one of those adamantine tendernesses which are the touchstones of every age and race. If other things are against it, other things must go down. If landlords and laws and sciences are against it, landlords and laws and sciences must go down. With the red hair of one she-urchin in the gutter I will set fire to all modern civilization. Because a girl should have long hair, she should have clean hair; because she should have clean hair, she should not have an unclean home: because she should not have an unclean home, she should have a free and leisured mother; because she should have a free mother, she should not have an usurious landlord; because there should not be an usurious landlord, there should be a redistribution of property; because there should be a redistribution of property, there shall be a revolution. That little urchin with the gold-red hair, whom I have just watched toddling past my house, she shall not be lopped and lamed and altered; her hair shall not be cut short like a convict's; no, all the kingdoms of the earth shall be hacked about and mutilated to suit her. She is the human and sacred image; all around her the social fabric shall sway and split and fall; the pillars of society shall be shaken, and the roofs of ages come rushing down, and not one hair of her head shall be harmed.